Navigating Your First Days
as a New Manager

NOW YOU'RE LEADING!

Raisa M. Ramos, MBA, SHRM-CP

Now You're Leading!

Navigating Your First Days as a New Manager

Copyright © 2025 by **Raisa M. Ramos.**

All rights reserved.

Published by: Find Joy Off The Path, LLC

ISBN: 979-8-9995490-1-3

Cover Design and Interior Formatting by 100Covers

No part of this book may be used, stored in a retrieval system, or transmitted by any means without the prior, written consent of the author, except as provided by the United States of America copyright law.

The information presented in Now You're Leading! Navigating Your First Days as a New Manager is intended solely for educational and informational purposes. It reflects the author's personal experiences and professional insights. Use of this book does not establish any kind of client relationship. If legal advice or expert assistance is required, the services of competent professionals should be sought. The author and publisher disclaim all liability for any loss, risk, or consequences, personal or professional, incurred directly or indirectly as a result of the use or misuse of this book's content. All trademarks, company names, and product names mentioned are the property of their respective owners. Reference to any organization, individual, or service does not constitute an endorsement.

Published in the United States of America

This is for Mami, the best cheerleader in the universe.

CONTENTS

Welcome to Leadership! 1

Week 1: Build Your Foundation for Success 7
    Day 1: Understand Your Role as a Manager 8
    Day 2: Meet Your Team (What to Ask & Listen For) 12
    Day 3: Assess Your Current Culture 17
    Day 4: Set Your Leadership Intentions 21
    Day 5: Learn From Your Predecessor 23
    Day 6: Identify Key Priorities 25
    Day 7: Weekly Reflection 27

Week 2: Relationships, Trust & Communication
Routines 31
    Day 8: Set the Tone in Your First Team Meeting 32
    Day 9: Learn Work Styles: Ask Questions
    That Build Trust 34
    Day 10: Recognize Team Strengths & Gaps 38
    Day 11: Understand Team Dynamics 41
    Day 12: Define Your Team Norms Together 45
    Day 13: Learn to "Manage Up" 47
    Day 14: Weekly Reflection 50

Week 3: Setting the Stage for Accountability,
Alignment & Autonomy 53
    Day 15: The Power of Clarity 54
    Day 16: Create & Align on Goals (Big + Small) 59
    Day 17: Delegate Without Micromanaging 65
    Day 18: Change Management 68
    Day 19: Give Feedback, Input & Guidance 70
    Day 20: Conflict 101 76
    Day 21: Weekly Reflection 83

Week 4: Grow Into Your Leadership Style 85
    Day 22: Develop Your Leadership Brand 86
    Day 23: Recognize Your Growth Edges 90
    Day 24: Define Healthy Boundaries 94
    Day 25: Seek Leadership Feedback 97
    Day 26: Lead With Authenticity 100
    Day 27: Celebrate Wins & Progress
    (Theirs + Yours) 102
    Day 28: Weekly Reflection 104

Week 5: Refocus & Realign for Self-Motivation 107
    Day 29: Finish Strong & Prepare for What's Next 108
    Day 30: Your 60 & 90-Day Roadmap 111

BONUS CHAPTER: Build Your Team
With Intention 116
The Final Decision 123
Final Thoughts: You Did It!!! 125
A Personal Note from Raisa 126
Keep Growing With Raisa 127
Acknowledgements 129
References 130

NOW YOU'RE LEADING!

Navigating Your First Days as a New Manager

WELCOME TO LEADERSHIP!

Congrats! If you're reading this, it means you've seized the opportunity to apply for a new internal or external position and are now a new manager. For others, it may be that the role was thrust upon you, but ultimately, your organization sees your talents and needs YOU. If these don't align with your situation, but you want to become a future leader – you're steps ahead, way to invest in yourself!

We all arrive at people leadership differently. You're here because you want to do your best, show up for your team, and show the mentors giving you this chance that their investment in you is worthwhile.

My first official role as a people leader was part of a rotational assignment. The introduction from my manager went something like this: *"Look Raisa, you have to understand something. You're going to be a 3rd shift maintenance supervisor. This is a group of thirty guys, most of them have been here over twenty years. You're a female, you're Hispanic, and truth be told, they simply don't want you."* You may be gasping or think this guy was a total jerk, but he wasn't. My manager and I had a really strong, positive working relationship. He was an excellent coach. We'd built rapport over the past year and spoke with each other candidly. My response was, *"Ok, I get it, I'm the underdog. But I'm not passing up the job. Where do I start?"* Here's what he said.

"They've already made a bunch of assumptions about you – but here's what they don't know. You're going to show them what I know you do best – build relationships. Before you know it, you'll win them over and make some real progress on 3rd shift like we've never seen before."

He was right. I used my strengths and got to know every single one of my team members. And not just them – the names of their kids, partners, what they did outside of work, and what they thought about working at this meat packing plant for over twenty years. I didn't know anything about hunting, but when they talked to me about their passion, and cooked venison for me, I joyfully ate it (it was delicious!). It was essentially the only workplace many of them knew. I wanted to learn from them, and I made it known. There was little sleep and long work hours, but the results made it all worthwhile.

When other supervisors sat with their feet propped at their desk after checking off their to-do's, I followed electricians, mechanics, millwrights, and plumbers around to learn different aspects of maintaining the plant. This was a union environment, so my being allowed to observe without associates putting up a huge stink with union leadership was a big deal. It meant they were starting to trust me.

My prior manager had been right and his advice paid off. I needed to hear the truth, and his encouragement, together. That was the first time I really understood what "employee engagement" meant before it even became the thing everyone talks about now. *You know how I measured success?* I had a guy on my team who had family and alcohol issues outside of work. He'd been caught several times on the job sleeping. One supervisor said to me early on, "*If he's caught again, he's fired.*"

Of course, he was also transferred to my department. Over a series of conversations, he finally reached out to our EAP (Employee Assistance Program) and got the help he desperately needed. A few months later, I organized a salsa-making contest for the plant for all three shifts. This gentleman not only participated but won 1st prize for best salsa! He was performing well on the job and became part of our team. People treated him differently and he thrived.

This was my wake-up call. I was a young engineer who would ultimately be expected to sit for hours in front of a computer designing and managing projects. But I knew in my heart that was not what I was meant to do. Eventually, I found my 'joy off the path' by seeking out opportunities that fulfilled my mission to help others advance and find their own joy.

As an HR Advisor and Leadership Coach, I've had the privilege of guiding numerous first-time and experienced managers on their leadership journey. The transition into a management role is both exciting and daunting. That's why I wrote this book, *Now You're Leading! Navigating Your First Days as a New Manager*, to provide you with real-life essential tools and strategies for navigating the challenges and opportunities that come with leading a team. These will help you cultivate the success that ultimately comes from investing in your people.

What to Expect in Your First Days

In the first days of assuming your new role, it's common to experience a variety of emotions, ranging from enthusiasm to uncertainty. Anyone who says differently is lying! Leadership is an ongoing journey; it's not always about making things perfect, but it is about showing up each day to be the best possible version of you, for your people. This book will help you build courage, providing you with a clear roadmap to understand your new role, build effective relationships with your team, and establish a strong leadership foundation.

Building Your Leadership Habits, One Day at a Time

This book is structured to provide you with a comprehensive framework for your first days as a people leader. While it's organized into a four-week journey, this guide is designed to give you a solid foundation, recognizing that true leadership is a continuous, lifelong pursuit.

Whether you're living out the first months of a new manager role or know that you need to re-set foundations with your team (and have prior leadership experience), this material is applicable across the board.

Each section addresses specific leadership aspects, from setting expectations and communicating effectively, to developing your team and fostering a positive work culture. These actionable insights will enable you to gain the mindset and skills needed to establish meaningful connections and lead your team with confidence.

End-of-Week Reflections

At the end of each week, you'll be met with a few reflection questions. To get the most out of this exercise, set aside an uninterrupted time block (15-30 minutes) and really think about what's transpired. *Schedule this on your calendar, mark it private, leave your office...do whatever you need to do – but don't skip this step!!!*

> **INSIGHT TIP:**
>
> *Keep a leadership journal. For those of you rolling their eyes...I'm not asking you to write a thesis – you don't have time for that! A few bullet points, one page per week is more than enough. This will be your powerful tool for self-awareness and growth.*

Trust me when I tell you this will be one of THE toughest good habits to develop as a new manager. Your daily to-do's will pile up faster than you can blink. You're going to need scheduled "thinking time" to reflect, strategize goals for your department, and plan how to approach critical conversations (and no, the *"my best thinking happens in the shower"* method won't cut it here).

Think long and hard before giving up that time to someone else when you're triple booked. It just so happens that everyone and their brother will decide to have an "emergency" that day.

If you break this promise to yourself now, the harder it will be to keep it in the coming weeks, and into your career.

Now that I'm off my soapbox...let's begin!

WEEK 1
Build Your Foundation for Success

DAY 1: UNDERSTAND YOUR ROLE AS A MANAGER

Welcome to your new chapter as a manager! Whether you were promoted internally or recently hired, stepping into a leadership role is exciting—and definitely a little intimidating. The best way to ground yourself is to start by understanding your true purpose.

Your Role Isn't Just to "Manage"—It's to Lead.

When I see a resume from a candidate applying to a people leader role that says, "I managed people", I automatically toss it aside. Managing is about organizing tasks. Leading is about inspiring people. Before you dive into the tactical elements of your new role, you've got to take a step back and understand what being a manager truly means.

As a manager, you're not just accountable for outcomes or overseeing tasks, but for creating the conditions that make success possible for your team. You're a coach, a motivator, a communicator, a decision maker, and a culture builder.

Does all that sounds daunting? You bet it does, and that's normal! Leaders aren't made overnight and they aren't perfect. What they are, is willing to show up day after day to learn, re-learn, and apply that knowledge to make today better than yesterday.

> **REFLECT**
>
> *Consider how your prior experiences (as a team member, colleague, or leader) have shaped your understanding of leadership.*
> *What type of manager do you want to be NOW?*
> *What's the kind of manager you NEVER want to be?*

> **TAKE ACTION**
>
> - Write down 3 specific expectations your supervisor has for you in this role. Not sure? Ask!
> - Job descriptions don't explain everything. Having clarity will help you understand your core responsibilities so you can start getting your arms around the circumstances.

The first week as a new manager is a whirlwind of emotions, new activities, and important decisions. It's easy to feel overwhelmed, but with the right approach, you can start strong and set the tone for a successful leadership journey. During your first week, you'll gain clarity on your role, meet your team, and establish the key intentions that will guide you through the rest of your first weeks and beyond.

Key Responsibilities to Embrace Early On

- **Get clear on your vision** as a leader and share it with your team
- **Set clear expectations** for performance and behavior
- **Align your team's work** with organizational goals

- **Support individual growth** and development
- **Foster a culture** of accountability and trust
- **Remove roadblocks** so your team can succeed

Yes, this is a big list. Take a breath, don't get overwhelmed. It's not meant to be done in a day, but they are key priorities you'll need to keep in front of you.

First thing's first: take 10 minutes today and jot down what kind of leader you want to be. Write it like a mission statement. Keep it visible — it'll anchor your decisions in the weeks to come.

Don't put it off because you're unclear — start with what you know! Don't let analysis paralysis or impostor syndrome get in your way. You have bigger fish to fry; you don't have time to let negative thoughts distract you. It's not a thesis and it's only for your eyes. You can come back as many times as you want to revisit and revise, but you've got to start today!

Here are some suggestions to get you started:

- I aspire to be the kind of leader who…
- I will lead with…
- My leadership is based on…
- I believe in open, respectful collaboration, positive intent…

My Leadership Mission Statement:

_____
_____
_____
_____

> **INSIGHT TIP:**
>
> *Embrace the mindset of a coach. While you'll still need to make decisions and guide your team, your focus should be on supporting and helping them grow.*

DAY 2: MEET YOUR TEAM (WHAT TO ASK & LISTEN FOR)

Before you dive into tasks and deadlines, connect with the people doing the work. Effective leaders take time to understand and get to know the people they're leading.

> **TAKE ACTION**
>
> Schedule one-on-ones (1:1s) with each team member this week. Let your team know these meetings are informal but intentional. Your goal today isn't to give direction—it's to learn.

Start with Weekly or Biweekly Meetings and adjust over time based on the team's needs. You can start with a simple format and dig deeper as time goes by.

Don't assume your team has been having ongoing 1:1s. These might have been a regular occurrence with their prior leader, or they may not even know what a 1:1 is – so ask them.

If I had a nickel for every time I've heard a leader say, *"I talk to my team daily, so we don't need to have 1:1s"*, I could've traveled to Hawaii and back twice now. Schedules fill up; there are customers, operations, sales, maintenance, marketing, HR, and so much more to care for. It's true; some days are genuinely overwhelming, but at the end of the day, that's just an excuse.

1:1s are your most powerful leadership tool. It's your team member's chance to speak with you individually, uninterrupted, privately. Daily check-in's and fly-by's don't take the place of a real 1:1. This is where you dive into career development, learn why your highest performer may be having a tough season, or talk about how to prepare for an upcoming challenge. If you leverage them wisely, 1:1 meetings build trust, catch problems early, and create a space for development conversations. **Don't let anyone convince you not to hold 1:1s with your team!**

> ### INSIGHT TIP:
>
> *If your team feels comfortable, let them own the 1:1 agenda. While you may need to lead those first ones, giving them ownership increases engagement and accountability.*
>
> *That said, if 1:1 meetings is a new concept, introducing my CAN-DO® format will give your team the confidence to know what they can come talk to you about in a 1:1.*

Questions to Ask in Your First 1:1s

Here are two examples of questions you can use for those first meetings, until you get an understanding of where everyone's comfort level is at:

Example 1 shares a key set of questions for your first meeting. After that, you can get more granular with **Example 2 and the CAN-DO© format**.

Example 1 - *Use a Simple Structure*

Leverage these questions to start creating dialogue:

- What's going well? What do you enjoy most about your role?
- What challenges are you facing?
- What's one thing you'd change if you could?
- How do you prefer to receive feedback or input?
- How can I support you? Any feedback for me and/or for the team? What can I Start, Stop, or Continue doing to help x, y, or z?

What to Listen For: What They Say & How They Say It

- Tone: Are they energized or burned out?
- Values: What motivates them? Look for insights into working styles, strengths, and pain points.
- Frustrations: What systems, processes, or dynamics may be causing friction?

Listening without jumping to fix things builds trust. Your goal isn't just to gather information but to build genuine rapport. It shows you care—and it helps you to evaluate the landscape and prepare to make better decisions. Maintain a positive, open, and collaborative tone. Pay attention to your posture and body language just as much as your tone.

Example 2 - *My proprietary CAN-DO© format.*

This is a way to present 1:1s with optimism and partnership, as opposed to a one-way conversation. You don't have to cover all the topics each time, but you'll always have something to talk about! No team member should ever say "*I have nothing to say*" during a 1:1.

C = Communication

- How are things going, how's life outside of work?
- Review examples of individual or team communication. Is there anything we should consider starting/stopping/continuing to improve our team culture?
- Specific concerns/questions you'd like to focus on?

A = Actions

- Wins for the week; best meeting you had, best personal development or team moment, etc.
- Update from last week's actions, timelines, and progress; roadblocks you need support with.
- What are your top priorities this week?

N = New Items

- Opportunity to share new items and updates, including communications, projects, accounts, processes, etc.

D = Development

- What skills do you want to work on? How are you stretching yourself in your current role?
- Are there other parts of the business you want to learn about or shadow?
- What are your long-term career goals? Do you know what paths are available?

O = Opportunities

- What feedback do you have (for me, team, process, etc.)? Improvements you'd like to propose.
- What can I do to support you or our team?
- What would you like to make sure we talk about next time?

Leverage **Example 2** once you've established increased rapport and can dive deeper into conversations with your team. Using the name "CAN-DO's" for meetings, as opposed to "1:1s" can also help to infuse positivity, if it's appropriate for your team's culture.

DAY 3: ASSESS YOUR CURRENT CULTURE

You inherited more than a position and team—you've inherited a culture. Culture is shaped by a variety of dynamics, including past leadership, internal processes, individual, and team experiences. It shows up in how people communicate, solve problems, give feedback, collaborate, and celebrate (or sadly ignore) wins.

Culture, Respect & Compliance

No matter what your company policies are, respect is the foundation of a healthy workplace culture. Respect should **ALWAYS** accompany your words, actions, and results. New managers often ask me for the "do's and don'ts" when it comes to HR compliance. We could write encyclopedias on those. Here, I'll focus on the "absolute do's" - and what you need to do if respect is lacking.

Absolute Do's: You're a leader, an advocate for upholding respect and ethics on your team and in your business – whether you're inside or outside its walls.

Respect means creating an environment where every individual feels valued and heard, regardless of their background, identity, or perspective. This commitment to respect extends to key compliance areas, ensuring that everyone adheres to a zero-tolerance policy for anti-harassment and discrimination.

By fostering a culture of mutual respect, diversity and equity, we don't just meet legal and ethical standards; we empower every team member to contribute their unique skills and ideas, leading to stronger collaboration, innovation, and a more inclusive environment for all.

Some behaviors that lack respect and may lead to further serious consequences if not managed properly, could include: continually dismissing others' opinions, making disrespectful or inappropriate jokes or comments about someone's appearance, background or personal life, bullying, spreading gossip or rumors, inappropriate touching, inconsistent application of rules or policies, taking credit for other people's work...this list isn't inclusive.

Any behavior listed above requires a conversation to bring awareness to the situation and those involved. See something, say something. **Don't** jump to conclusions about how serious it will or won't be. **Don't** make your own judgments. **Don't** dismiss what may seem small.

Your responsibility is to take the next best step. You may not know what that is, and that's ok. Sometimes it means:

- Seeking out your leader for advice,
- Talking to HR for awareness and guidance,
- Giving feedback to bring awareness to the situation,
- Having an open dialogue about respect; what's ok and what's not ok,
- Following company policy on anti-harassment,
- Calling an anonymous company ethics hotline...

The bottom line is simple - respect should always be honored. There are situations that can severely and quickly get out of control if mismanaged. If you don't know what to do, call HR to lead you in the right direction. Ask for help!

When we know that our compliance priorities are in check, then we can go deeper to learn about culture.

Take Action
• Take a "walk" through your team's environment (whether that's physical or virtual). Observe how people interact with each other, what kind of language is used, and how decisions are made. Reflect on the overall mood and morale. • Sit in on team meetings (without leading them) • Ask "How do we usually handle ___?" or "What do we do when___?" • Notice how people speak to each other—formally or casually? Open or guarded? Who do they look to?

Reflect
• What do people seem proud of here? • What's not being said out loud but seems important? • Are people solving problems or avoiding them? • What's the level of trust within the team? • What values seem to guide day-to-day work?

Be careful – it's not time to judge what you find—just take inventory. Practice assuming positive intent (*e.g., **make*** *the conscious choice to believe someone is acting with good intentions, even if you think they show the opposite... first, seek to understand.)* Awareness is the first step to learning and shaping the culture you want to grow. Write down your observations!

INSIGHT TIP:

Culture is built on small, repetitive, daily behaviors. If you can identify what's working well, you can amplify those behaviors. If something needs to change, start small by modeling the behaviors you want to see.

DAY 4: SET YOUR LEADERSHIP INTENTIONS

Great leaders don't just react—they lead with intention. Today is about setting the tone for your team. Now that you've spent a couple days with your team, let's revisit the Leadership Mission Statement you wrote on Day 1.

Think about it like this: *What do I want to accomplish in the next 30 days?*

TAKE ACTION
Complete this sentence: "As a leader, I want to be known for…" Write down **3 qualities or principles** you want to embody (e.g., fairness, clarity, approachability). 1. _____ 2. _____ 3. _____ **Then Ask Yourself:** • *How will I demonstrate these values?* • *What boundaries will I need to protect them?* • *How will I hold myself accountable?*

INSIGHT TIP:

Intentional leadership builds trust. Share your Leadership Mission Statement and your vision with your team. Let them know what they can expect from you and how you plan to lead.

When people know and see what they can expect from you, they'll feel safe and empowered. That's genuine leadership, and it will build a bridge of trust early on.

Feel weird saying "Team, this is my Leadership Mission Statement"?

Try this: "Team, I know we're just getting to know each other. As we grow this will evolve. I want you to know that as your leader, I'll strive to act with (insert 3 qualities or principles here) as we work to achieve our goals of (name 2-3 specific goals or a more department-specific goal 'to become the go-to resource for Customer Service questions'.)

DAY 5: LEARN FROM YOUR PREDECESSOR

If someone held the role before you, reach out or review notes, files, or project histories to understand their legacy.

If you can speak with your predecessor, ask:

- What worked well under your leadership?
- What were the biggest challenges you faced?
- How did you navigate difficult decisions or conflicts?
- What does the team need at this point?
- What advice do you have for me?
- How can I foster a positive relationship with my team, peers, leader, and key stakeholders?

If you can't speak with them, ask your leader, peers, and team members:

- What worked well under their leadership that you would like to see continue?
- What would you have liked them to start doing?
- What left people frustrated or unclear?
- Are there goals that have been delayed or ignored? Were there circumstances that impacted this?

You're forming a picture of current state. This doesn't mean you need to replicate their style—no matter how incredible of a leader they were. The take-away here is that understanding their impact will help you sustain implemented best practices that work well, avoid unintentional landmines, and identify areas for growth.

If you're replacing a beloved leader, don't go insane comparing yourself to them. Instead, honor their behaviors and results. If you're replacing an ineffective manager, build trust first and create a fresh start.

> ### Insight Tip:
>
> *If your predecessor left under less-than-ideal circumstances and their legacy isn't admired, it may be tougher than expected, but you can do hard things.*
>
> *Focus on what you can learn from their mistakes – what you don't want to repeat. Don't badmouth or blame them, especially in front of your team.*
>
> *Remember, you're creating a culture that elevates attitudes above the norm. Every person is a teacher if we choose to see them that way.*

DAY 6: IDENTIFY KEY PRIORITIES

Now that you've taken the steps to listen and observe, it's time to focus. You can't fix everything at once. There will be a hundred different things you want to fix, but Rome wasn't built in a day. You won't impress anyone, and you'll end up having the opposite effect, even when you had good intentions.

Your key priorities should be aligned with the goals of your team and the larger organization.

Let's identify priorities by focusing on the 3P Method:

1. **People:** Who needs support, recognition, or feedback?
2. **Processes:** What's broken or inefficient?
3. **Performance:** What are the critical goals to hit this month, quarter, or year?

Pick 1 to 3 small target wins you can deliver in the next 30 days. No more! Break each priority into smaller, actionable tasks so they don't feel overwhelming.

Focus on the most critical priorities first. Fight every single urge you get to do more than you can realistically handle.

Will things get in the way? Yes.

Will another emergency hit the fan? Yes.

Will you feel like you can't solve one thing without having three more problems pop up? Yes.

Slow and steady wins the race. Keep persisting. Momentum builds credibility. Examples of wins include:

improving communication by having a weekly staff meeting, aligning the team on shared goals, completing your first 1:1s, or holding a team lunch to get to know each other.

Take Action
Write My Target Wins for the Next 30 Days Win 1 will be: Win 2 will be: Win 3 will be:

DAY 7: WEEKLY REFLECTION

You've succeeded! With these first days under your belt, it's time to pause and check in with yourself. Think about what you've learned. Reflection is essential to your development; make it a part of your regular, personal practice.

TAKE ACTION
Set aside 30 minutes each week on your calendar to reflect. *This is an actual appointment you need to add in your calendar with yourself.* **Beware!** This will be the first slot to be triple booked on your calendar. Without a doubt, your manager, your team, or an esteemed peer will want to meet with you at this time. You'll quickly hit the easy button and say "Sure, I can just move that." **WRONG!** If you don't start developing this habit now, it won't get any easier later. Manage your calendar or someone else will manage it for you!

Find a place where you can reflect without being disturbed. Take out your leadership journal and answer the following:

> ## Reflect
>
> - *What went really well this week? What energized me?*
>
> - *What surprised me this week?*
>
> - *What drained me? What challenges did I face, and how did I handle them?*
>
> - *What could I have done differently this week?*
>
> - *What's one leadership habit I want to carry forward into next week?*

Use this reflection as a learning opportunity. If something didn't go as planned, don't beat yourself up! You did the best you could at the time with what you knew. Learn, pivot, and ask yourself what you can do differently next time.

✓ **Takeaway for Week 1:**

You're laying the foundation of your leadership. By listening deeply, setting intentions, and clarifying your role, you've already started building trust. Keep showing up with curiosity and courage—you've got this!

Conclusion

Your first seven days as a manager have been all about laying your leadership foundation. You've taken the time to understand your role, meet your team, evaluate culture, and define your leadership mission statement. As you move forward, keep building on these fundamentals by staying connected to your team, remaining adaptable, and continuing to reflect on your progress.

These first steps are critical, but they are just the beginning. The following weeks will bring new challenges and opportunities. You won't yet be ready to tackle all of them – and that's ok.

What you will be doing is building your courage muscle. Keep going.

WEEK 2

Relationships, Trust & Communication Routines

DAY 8: SET THE TONE IN YOUR FIRST TEAM MEETING

Your first team meeting is THE golden opportunity to set the tone for how you'll lead and how you want the team to work together. It's less about updates and more about connection.

Tips for an Impactful First Team Meeting

- Keep it short (30 minutes or less). If you're able to provide food, do it! Having a snack or lunch helps put people at ease.
- Share your leadership intentions and style. Outline your 'ground rules'.
- Invite the team to share what's important to them.
- Make sure everyone feels included. If you have remote team members, turn on your cameras so they can see everyone. If your team is remote, make it a habit to turn on cameras; create a culture of connection. You can adjust as you go, but in the beginning it will be especially critical for strengthening connections.
- Reinforce that your goal in these first weeks is to listen, learn, and support.

Here's a Sample Opening Script

"Hello everyone, it's great to be here with all of you today! I'd like to take a few minutes to introduce myself not just

as your manager, but as a partner who's here to learn and help this team thrive. I'm here to support your success, understand what's working, and remove roadblocks. I don't pretend to know everything, I'm here to learn. I do believe in open communication, mutual respect, and continuous improvement."

This is just a sample to get you started. If it doesn't align with your style and your voice, just change it! You get the idea. You're not expected to have all the answers—just lead with openness and follow-through.

To ALL leaders who start working with a new team (whether you're new or experienced), ask your HR department to facilitate a **New Team Integration Session.** If your HR team isn't familiar with this, contact me at raisa@findjoyoffthepath.com to learn more.

Unlike anything you've experienced before, this interactive workshop is a catalyst for meaningful team transformation, relieving doubts, reducing turnover, and decreasing a new manager's ramp-up time by 50%!

Through expert facilitation, this activity unites new leaders and their teams, creating a safe, fun, and engaging space to ask crucial questions that when left unanswered cause confusion, missed expectations, and distrust. The session should be held within a leader's first 30 days, as soon as possible.

Whether you're a new leader joining a new company, new to management internally, or an experienced leader joining a new team, I can't overstate how invaluable this session will be for you and your new team.

DAY 9: LEARN WORK STYLES: ASK QUESTIONS THAT BUILD TRUST

Every person works differently. Excellent leaders understand this and adapt to each style. Start learning how each person prefers to operate and think about how you can flex to meet them where they're at.

Ask Informal Questions in 1:1s or Team Chats

- How do you like to receive feedback?
- Do you prefer emails, chats, or quick calls?
- What's your favorite way to stay organized?

Look for Context Clues

- Do they ask for structure or figure it out as they go?
- Do they work best solo or with others?
- Do they thrive on praise or autonomy?
- Do they prefer individual or broad recognition?

These signs will help you tailor your approach, reduce friction, and motivate each person in a way that resonates with them and feels real.

Who's Your Primary Team?

If you re-read this section from the top, it's assumed I'm talking about your direct reports. I am, but it's not just them.

When you become a leader, especially for the first time, your immediate focus naturally shifts to your direct reports. And rightly so! But here's a crucial insight that often gets overlooked: your true "primary team" as a manager is often your peer group of fellow managers.

Why? Because while you lead your direct reports, you manage through your peers. This also extends to stakeholders. Think about it…

Cross-functional collaboration: Most significant initiatives require seamless work across different teams. Your ability to influence, negotiate, and collaborate effectively with your fellow managers directly impacts your team's ability to achieve its goals.

Shared challenges: Who best understands the unique struggles of managing people, navigating organizational politics, or pushing through difficult projects? Your peers. They're your sounding board, your source of innovative solutions, and your emotional support system.

Organizational influence: Want to advocate for your team, push for a new process, or secure resources? You'll often need the collective power and alignment of your managerial peers to make significant organizational changes happen.

Personal growth: Your peers can offer candid feedback, mentorship, and diverse perspectives that accelerate your own leadership development in ways your direct reports simply can't.

Make it a priority to invest in these connections – share insights, offer support, and build trust. They are your leverage, your allies, and your most valuable resource in navigating the complexities of leadership.

Influence Without Authority

Influencing peers, customers, stakeholders – and leaders more senior than you – is the ability to guide, motivate, and rally others toward a common goal without having formal authority over them.

The relationships you're building beyond your team matter more than you realize. Exerting influence without authority relies on your capabilities to establish credibility, build trust, show empathy, and actively listen. The result is an elevated kind of respect, the kind that leads to unique collaboration and true buy-in to resolve the most complex of issues. This skill isn't just reserved for people leaders. In time you'll become more proficient, and more importantly teach your team how to foster the qualities that build influence without authority.

Emotional Intelligence

Emotional intelligence (EI) is the ability to understand and manage your own emotions, as well as to recognize and influence the emotions of those around you.

As important as it is to learn about others' work styles, being self-aware will allow you to control your reactions to stress and tension, helping you prevent impulsive decisions and maintain a calm demeanor for yourself and others.

Recognizing the emotions of your team, whether it's frustration with a project or excitement about a contract win, allows you to respond with empathy and provide the right support. This fosters trust and psychological safety, essential for a team to communicate openly, take measured risks, and collaborate effectively. Leaders with high emotional intelligence win over expert leaders on a particular product, process, or service. They do more than create positive and productive environments; they transform individuals into cohesive and resilient teams.

DAY 10: RECOGNIZE TEAM STRENGTHS & GAPS

In these first days, you're making observations about people and circumstances. Listen and observe everything around you. Pay close attention to verbal and non-verbal behaviors.

- What do individuals love to do? What are they really good at?
- How does your team collaborate?
- Is everyone on the team equipped with the knowledge to do their job?
- How is stress managed?
- How do they learn new skills?
- How do individuals among the team communicate? In sub-groups? With others outside the team?

You can think about this by using the SWOT analysis technique to identify internal and external factors that influence individual and team performance. Here's what SWOT means:

- S = What are the **inner strengths and advantages** that give them a competitive edge?
- W = What are the **internal limitations** that can potentially hinder their progress?
- O = What **external factors or environment** can they leverage for success?
- T = What **external factors or environment** negatively impacts their work?

This week is all about observation. Pay attention to signs such as tone, body language, and attitudes. Look for patterns that will give you insights into the learning agility and adaptability of each team member. If you haven't focused this much on observing people before, you'll be quite surprised at what you can learn, and what different situations will reveal!

Identifying Gaps

It's absolutely gut-wrenching to watch an individual or team struggle due to skill, knowledge, or process gaps. It's even tougher to talk to someone about their weaknesses, behaviors, or the lack of skills holding them back. It's still a conversation you need to have, with kindness and respect.

Our strengths are well-functioning muscles that naturally excel at their purpose. Sometimes, weaknesses and derailers at one point may have even been someone's strengths, but perhaps now are being overused. This analogy has helped me during difficult conversations to keep the focus on the skill and the behavior we want to adjust, never berating the person, but helping to explain the balance between the two.

We may indeed fully overcome certain weak spots with conscious effort, time, and practice. Some of us may always need a little extra focus to make sure we stay in check. Your job as the leader is to help bring awareness of both and help your team find equilibrium.

Most importantly, coach your team be vulnerable. Yes, you heard me, vulnerable. The strongest teams are those that know who rocks at which "thing". They celebrate it, set their egos aside, and go to directly to the source for help. Strong teams simply don't have the time, energy, or resources to waste. They know how to lean and leverage each other, to achieve team excellence. This doesn't mean "passing the buck" on accountability; it means following through and collaborating, by working smarter, not harder.

Your team needs to know what their joint strengths and weaknesses are. They need to be brave enough to seek each other out for genuine support. If you can teach them this, you'll teach them to conquer any set of circumstances they encounter.

DAY 11: UNDERSTAND TEAM DYNAMICS

Team culture goes beyond an individual's motivations — it's how people interact as peers, teams, and broader organization. Culture is engrained in how communication flows and decisions are made.

Watch for:

- Who dominates conversations? Who stays quiet?
- How does the team interact as peers? Are there 'quiet leads' in the group?
- Is there mutual respect, or passive resistance?
- Are issues raised openly or buried?
- Is there specific body language you see that supports certain behaviors?
- Do people feel open and at ease to express their opinions?

Ask Privately (When Appropriate)

This can be tricky because you want to learn more information but be careful not to give the impression that you're playing 'favorites' with anyone or trying to gossip. You could choose to let the team know you'll be asking them similar questions both in team meetings and in 1:1s as you get to know everyone better over your first few weeks.

Some examples you can use include:

- What do you think helps this team collaborate best?
- What do you love most about our team?
- What could improve how we work together?
- If you had a magic wand and could change one thing, what would that be?

Keep actively listening. Map out dynamics without judgment. The better you understand the unwritten rules and informal systems, the better you'll be able to lead the formal ones.

Another way to gain insight into team dynamics and personalities are considering assessments that can help you and the team understand more about one another, and why they approach situations differently. The DiSC®, Myers-Briggs Type Indicator® (MBTI®), and Clifton StrengthsFinder® assessments are just a few of a wide variety of options that offer different approaches to understanding personalities, talents, and behavioral tendencies.

Building Psychological Safety

I'm sure you've heard the saying "People don't leave companies, they leave managers." The best leaders are the ones who foster an inclusive environment, who listen, and respect everyone's opinions – and teach others to do so by their example.

What is Psychological Safety?

Don't let the term scare you away; it's not about getting all touchy feely. This is about making people feel genuinely safe to speak up without fear of being punished or embarrassed. Emotional safety is the absence of interpersonal fear; believing that you're accepted for who you are and what you bring to the table, without reproach or judgment. That's how you build a strong foundation with people who will do anything to support you and each other. Start cultivating that now.

How to Build Emotional Safety as a People Leader

- Be honest. Say "*I don't know*" when you don't.
- If you can't share confidential information say, "*I can't share that at this time, but I'll tell you as much as I can, as soon as I'm able to.*"
- Ask, "*What am I missing?*"
- Thank people for their honesty—even if it feels uncomfortable in that moment.
- Don't beat around the bush—admit when you make a mistake.
- Ask for help and coach your team to do the same. If you don't model it, they won't do it.

The goal isn't perfection—it's trust. It also doesn't mean agreeing with everyone, but it does mean acknowledging that each person on your team has a gift to share. When every person on the team recognizes that and becomes vulnerable enough to ask for and offer help, then you've become a real team.

When people feel safe with you—whether they directly report to you or not—they'll show up fully and do their best work. That last part is important. Just because you're a leader, doesn't mean everyone reports to you. Your influence and reach with others will make a difference in the big picture goals your team and your organization are focused on.

While we're focusing on all the aspects of building your team, remember that there will be others around you who are watching, and will also be impacted by your leadership example. You are becoming a servant leader.

What is a Servant Leader?

A servant leader is a leader who is genuinely focused on serving the team, not having the team serve them. It's when a leader prioritizes the growth, empowerment, and needs of their people, truly acting as a coach and mentor, as opposed to a commander and dictator.

Servant leaders build psychological safety naturally because they create environments where people feel confident enough to be themselves. Show me a team who feels they can share their opinions, ask questions, and challenge the status quo without fear of being judged or reprimanded, and surely enough a servant leader will have been the reason the team is thriving.

On the days when you're searching for ways to build psychological safety on your team, think about which people in your life are servant leaders. They may not have a manager or executive title, yet their actions, words, and results are what draw others to them. Observing and speaking with them will give you insightful clues on how to take steps to becoming a servant leader yourself.

DAY 12: DEFINE YOUR TEAM NORMS TOGETHER

What's the best way to form camaraderie and build positive team culture? Invite your team in. Instead of imposing rules, co-create team agreements. This empowers people and fosters ownership. When a team aligns on their values, their mission and their purpose, a shared sense of accountability and empowerment is created.

As you and your team continue to define your norms, be honest with one another, especially in those tough moments when any one of you may stray from your values. Keep strengthening your bonds. Without a doubt, others outside your function will notice and start asking, *"What are they doing differently from our team?"*

Starting the Conversation

Get your team engaged. This is a great opportunity for a group activity during your team meeting. Ask:

- What makes a great team experience?
- How do we want to celebrate wins?
- How should we handle conflict?
- What do we want to be known for in our organization? How do we want others to "see" us?

Write a Team Charter with 4-6 norms, such as:

- Our team assumes positive intent first, which means we don't jump to conclusions until we better understand the circumstances.
- We default to over-communicating and asking open-ended questions to encourage dialogue.
- We ask who needs help in our meetings.
- We keep meetings respectful and productive.
- We don't let things fester – we find productive ways to manage conflict.
- We celebrate individual and team wins – both professional and personal.

Post it. Live it. Refer to it often. Consider reading your team charter or mission as the intro to your team meetings and keep it top of mind.

DAY 13: LEARN TO "MANAGE UP"

What do people mean when they say, 'managing up'? This refers to the process of effectively and proactively managing the relationship with your leader. Historically, the phrase has a negative connotation, assuming that a manager has an 'unmanageable' style and because of it, you need to be in constant defense mode. It also implies employees may likely need to steer away from or even worse — manipulate their boss to convince them to get what they want. Ugh. That's an awful way to live at work.

Let me really clear – no one builds positive relationships with their manager (or anyone) with this mentality. There will be times in your career when you'll have constructive and passionate conversations with your manager. You won't be in agreement, and you may need to agree to disagree or take a breath and reconvene. And while I hope you never work for an ogre, I'm not naïve; I know they exist. Sadly, I've worked for them too and because of it have learned what NOT to do.

At some point, you're going to have disagreements with your manager – especially if you're both deeply invested in your work and your people. The way to get through these challenging moments is to prioritize and respect your working relationship above any issue. When you keep the respect you have for each other in high regard, you can come to a resolution or at minimum, an understanding of why things need to proceed the way they do.

However, if you're in a situation with a manager where constant defense is your survival MO, that's completely unhealthy. Evaluate for yourself what kind of leader they are by carefully observing their words and actions. Is this the mentor you want to work with? If you're in a situation where you want to hide, run, or scream when you see your leader, you really need to assess what's going on.

This isn't an endorsement for impulsive moves, such as delivering an ultimatum, having a tantrum, or orchestrating a department-wide, full-blown, Rogue One-style rebellion. However, if your manager's values clash with your own, (and likely the organization's), it's time to carefully evaluate your path forward.

Managing up is about being a partner to your leader. "What, really?" Yes. Think of yourself as the solution to your manager's challenges, questions, and at times, even unstated needs. It's normal not to know everything; when you don't, proactively seek out the answers. Always follow up and follow through. Show your commitment by actively engaging to be part of the solution, not the problem.

Tips to Build a Strong Relationship with Your Leader

- Leave your assumptions and judgment at the door. Realize that you only have a small glimpse into your manager's responsibilities and challenges. Be supportive but be careful of making big statements when you don't have full context.
- Ask about their priorities, goals, and how you and your team can help achieve them.
- Communicate early and often – never let your manager be surprised. And I do mean never. If you feel

something isn't right, give them an early warning sign. It's always better to provide awareness than for problems to explode later.
- Understand the foundational KPIs (Key Performance Indicators), e.g., how does your leader and the organization measure progress? Are there targets that need to be met? By when? What happens if you can't meet them? What's the process for partnering with your leader, peers and stakeholders prior, before disaster slams down your door?
- Come prepared for meetings; know what's on the agenda and what's expected so you can contribute. Ask questions to help clarify understanding.
- Develop empathetic listening.
- Ask your manager about their communication preferences; text, email or phone call, when they have the ability to be most responsive, how to best get ahold of them during an urgent situation, etc.
- Ask regularly *"How am I meeting your expectations?"*
- Don't dump a problem on your manager's doorstep. Even when you're stumped, the best thing to do is to re-state the situation. Present a couple of potential options or explain why you're uncertain of which one would be best. While you may not have the final answer, showing that you made a genuine attempt will earn you big bonus points.

DAY 14: WEEKLY REFLECTION

Week 2 is in the books! You're still getting the lay of the land. Likely drinking heavily from the firehouse, trying to come up for air. It's ok. Trust me, you're not alone.

Having heart-pounding moments while figuring out what the next best step is, sometimes on a daily basis or hour by the hour, is a real thing. Don't let present challenges cloud your vision for long-term success. BREATHE, you got this!

Yes, there's as many daily challenges as menu options at your favorite restaurant. Good leaders learn in time to balance; they give their best at the present time with the resources they have and then make tomorrow better.

Remember: you're in this role because YOU have the talent, commitment, and drive to make things better than what they are today. Time to take out your journal.

> **REFLECT**
>
> - *What did I learn about my team's working styles this week?*
>
> - *What do I know about my leader so far? How could I be a partner to them?*
>
> - *What can I continue, or try differently next week?*

> **INSIGHT TIP:**
>
> *Ask your team what they need more or less of from you. It shows courage and humility, that you continue to show up as a student—and creates a culture of feedback.*

✓ Takeaway for Week 2:

You're building connections; with your team, leaders, and peers. Trust is growing. Communication is opening. Your team is starting to understand who you are—and you're learning about them too. Taking one small, meaningful action, every day, will bring you closer to positive, broader-impact results. You're not sprinting here; this is a marathon—pace yourself.

WEEK 3

Setting the Stage for Accountability, Alignment & Autonomy

DAY 15: THE POWER OF CLARITY

Being clear with people, using the right approach, shows respect and professional kindness. Setting clear expectations begins with a review of roles and responsibilities. Clear roles prevent duplication, confusion, and dropped balls. Confirm who owns what and where overlap exists. Asking about people's jobs will naturally create doubt and uncertainty, but you've got to follow-through and talk about responsibilities. Explaining your positive intent and "why" will help set the stage for transparency.

Over the past two weeks you've focused on building relationships; expectations plays a huge role here. Setting expectations feels scary at first, but it's an important ingredient for strong relationships. Why? Because just like friends want to know where they stand with one another, so do your team members. A good majority of humans innately want to do their best and want someone (you!) to notice their hard work.

Clarifying responsibilities shows you're invested in understanding your team's work, but more importantly, that you really know what their talents are, and how they're applying them, or not, if it turns out they're being underutilized. This will give you clues into individual and team performance, and how to continue motivating your team—a powerful way to retain talent. To gain a better understanding of the different roles on your team…

Take Action

Review your team's job descriptions and compare them to *what people actually do*. If something isn't accurate, correct it!

If a job description doesn't exist, create one! It sounds logical, but you'd be surprised. Set time aside with each person on your team. Leverage this opportunity to shadow team members, learn, and show a genuine interest in what they do. Even if job descriptions exist, make time for shadowing—it's an essential investment you'll never regret.

Use team meetings to talk about collective processes. Taking the time to map these out from end-to-end is **ALWAYS** worthwhile.

Even if processes are 'already documented', you and your team might be surprised by what you learn. **Ask: *"What's something you're responsible for that others may not realize?"*** This creates opportunity to let them lead and explain their collective expertise to you. Clarify gray areas and handoffs. Capture these outcomes on a joint platform and make them readily accessible for all.

> ### INSIGHT TIP:
>
> *As you start talking about job descriptions, you're going to hear feedback and questions about compensation from your team.* **Don't get nervous!** *Listen; let them know you're here to learn and understand the overall state of the team. Don't make promises or lead individuals to believe they'll get a raise – learn first.*
>
> *You need to know how much everyone earns, their PTO or vacation balance, etc. If you see discrepancies in responsibilities vs. pay, meet with your HR department. Ask for additional information and history around salary ranges and position grades.*
>
> *If salaries aren't aligning with duties, work with HR and your leader to make planned salary adjustments. Don't assume business conditions can support a $10k jump, but you can propose thoughtful plans to make changes that show you're a leader who understands the perspective of the employee and the company.*
>
> **Don't share confidential salary information or make promises about increases until they're finalized. Follow your company's guidelines and never assume – ASK!**

Clarity Builds Accountability

The #1 misunderstanding among managers and teams is about expectations and performance. The bottom line is your team can't read your mind. Review what you say and how you say it. Ask open-ended questions. Let them repeat what you said back to them.

No matter how bright people are, they simply can't assume how they should present materials to you, or how you want them to prepare for meetings. Let's take a moment to define what high performance means to you, and how you want to articulate that.

You could say…

"Team, I'd like to share with you what my expectations are of how we'll work together. These will help us stay on the same page, and in time, we'll grow more in-sync. We're learning each other's styles, and I welcome any questions you have as we do so." Then, state your expectations.

Here's a few examples to spark your own ideas:

- Be solution-oriented when raising problems.
- Deliver work on time—or give a heads-up if you can't and explain why.
- Come to our 1:1s prepared with topics that are important to you.
- Treat all colleagues with respect, especially during disagreements.
- I'm fine with drafts—please send them to me a week before the final is due so I can provide feedback.
- Please share bad news with me as soon as possible. I prefer a [*you insert your preferred methods: phone call, text, or face-to-face talk*] if possible. Where you can, don't let me be surprised.
- If you're unsure of how to handle an issue, let's talk. Asking for help isn't a sign of weakness, it's a chance for us to learn together.

Think about your tone, words, and frame up an encouraging message. Invite input from the team to check that your message is understood.

Based on past negative experiences, many people tend to equate accountability with managers talking down to them and instilling fear of making mistakes. Autocratic leaders leverage fear because they're terrified to trust anyone but themselves. This results in self-destructive cultures where business results become stagnant and suffer. That is NOT the kind of leader you're striving to be.

Real accountability is knowing that we're marching towards common goals. Each person brings their talents and skills to achieve them. It's about a shared value of respect among a team and their leader, to hold each other responsible to the promises they've made to one another. You respect each other, and therefore, don't want to break that commitment.

When your expectations as a leader are clear, and you exercise follow-through, you demonstrate accountability. If you want your team to be accountable, you've got to show up first. This means:

- *You follow up on requests on their due date,*
- *You follow up with answers when you committed,*
- *You complete an action from last week's 1:1…*

Every single activity you finish shows that you hold accountability in high regard.

Even if you have a million problems to solve in your department right now, one small single act, every day will build the culture of accountability you'll need to solve bigger, future problems.

DAY 16: CREATE & ALIGN ON GOALS (BIG + SMALL)

People want to know: *"What are we aiming for?"* Kickstart your goal-setting today. Form a plan to align with your leader on company goals. When you're 100% clear on the targets, you can articulate them to your team and strategize actionable steps to get there.

Critical Tips on Goal Setting & Measuring Progress

At this point your leader may have already "given" you the team's goals but bear with me. After everything you're absorbing, it's worthwhile to revisit. Consistently reviewing your goals is important, to make sure you're on track. The first step to creating (or re-stating) goals is breaking them down into objectives that are achievable and clear. You've got a ton on your plate; the name of the game is to work SMARTer, not harder. Pun purposely intended.

SMART Goals

The SMART Goal format aims to provide a straightforward framework to 'proof' your goals; to see if they hold water and are legitimately feasible. Once your leader communicates what you'll be accountable for, review the objectives carefully and see if they pass this test. Can you break them down into the SMART goal format? If yes, great! Then you're ready to communicate broadly with your team and break down activities further as needed. But if something doesn't match up, stop and don't take another step! Go back and clarify before sharing further. Why? Because if you can't understand 100% of the objectives, you can't fully buy into them. You won't be able to advocate for them or gain buy-in from anyone else, let alone answer questions from your team. People will see through it faster than you can blink.

Here's the SMART Goal breakdown:

Specific: *Define and clearly state the goal. Instead of "improved customer relations", opt for "10% increase in customer satisfaction."*

Measurable: *You need to be able to track progress, which is achieved by quantifying the goal. I realize there are times where this is easier said than done, but you'll need to challenge yourself and find ways to measure.* **Don't take the easy way out!**

Achievable: *Realistic and attainable for your team. If your team is less experienced, be patient as their skills develop. In time, you'll have the ability to give them stretch goals.*

Relevant: *The goal must align with the company's objectives and the team's purpose; it must be clear to them how they impact the bigger mission.*

Timely: *Steer clear of open-ended objectives! Set a clear deadline and explain the level of urgency for every goal.*

Here's two examples:

Example 1: At ABC Company, our goal is to improve our customer satisfaction score from 70% to 80% by the end of

Q3 by implementing two innovative training programs: one for our customers, and one for our internal customer team.

Example 2: Within the next fiscal year, we're going to increase manager retention by 10% by launching a focused leadership development program in Q2, which includes a formal mentorship program that pairs each new manager with an experienced leader for 1 meeting each month and developing a personal career development plan with HR for the next 12 months.

Measuring Progress

Let's go back to the 'Measuring' piece before we talk about aligning with your leader. This will help you prepare for that conversation. When new managers think about measuring progress, it's scary to think you're "keeping tabs on people". Measuring progress isn't about instilling fear. It's about holding ourselves together, as a team, accountable to our team culture. It means knowing when we're succeeding so we can celebrate small wins and help each other through stumbling blocks.

The reason we're tackling this on Day 16 is because first, you focus on relationships, build rapport, and establish the team mission. When you've taken a few steps forward there, now you can go deeper into goal-setting.

Remember what I said before? People want to know where they stand. It's all about approach. You and your team are on a mission to enhance what you do today. I challenge you: don't just 'make it better', 'make it the best'. When a business succeeds, every person thrives, professionally and personally. Measuring progress is about quantity and quality. Some different tools you can consider to measure and share progress include: reports, focus groups, project management tools, specific project checkpoints, visual boards, etc.

Aligning With Your Leader

Just like you've been having 1:1s with your team – you need to do the same with your leader. Ideally, your manager should initiate 1:1s with you. That said – it may not always happen that way. Ultimately, YOU own your development. 1:1s are a part of your development, so if they haven't scheduled them yet, take the initiative to DIY.

Don't start spiraling into doubts about their leadership style. Negative thinking isn't going to help you. First, assume positive intent. Then, follow-up. Your manager may be struggling with issues that you're unaware of, which is why scheduling has been delayed. Or... you may be right and sadly this wasn't on their priority list when it should've been. If you needed to hear it, I just told you. Great managers make sure their directs, especially leaders of people, and leaders of leaders, are set up for success.

INSIGHT TIP:

If this doesn't happen how it should, take the next best step. You're here to make a positive impact. You can't do that without clarity from your leader. If that clarity isn't being readily available to you as it should, figure out how to find it. You can do this.
Send them an invite. Don't overthink it. If they have conflicts, they can propose an alternate time. Make it easy for you both! This will show your leader that you prioritize aligning with their mission and company goals.

TAKE ACTION

Ask your manager: *"What are our top 3 priorities this quarter?"* Re-state their response so that you walk away with equal understanding. Bring the SMART goal format with you.

I've always found the question *"Who will do what by when?"*, also an excellent book by Tom Hanson and Birgit Zacher Hanson, to be incredibly helpful to verify that accountabilities are understood by both parties.

We all want to look competent at our jobs, especially as a new leader! That doesn't mean you should just robotically nod your head when hearing the objectives. Be brave; asking a few follow-up questions will help you walk away with a clear understanding of what you're responsible for.

Next, translate priorities into team objectives. Ask yourself:

- *Am I explaining the objectives in a way that is clear to the team?*
- *Do we need to break down bigger milestones into smaller activities?*
- *Did I clarify the milestones, KPIs, checkpoints, and deadlines?*
- *How will they know if they're doing well or not?*
- *Have I asked my team to re-state them back to me? Did we all arrive at the same understanding?*

Collaborate with each person to set short-term, achievable goals that support the big picture. Be open to questions and uncertainty.

Remember, this may be the first time anyone has ever actually explained to your team what the objectives are, and how each member plays an important role in overall results.

Even if goals shift later due to changing circumstances, this builds direction and purpose. It doesn't need to be perfect, just start.

DAY 17: DELEGATE WITHOUT MICROMANAGING

"A boss who micromanages is like a coach who wants to get in the game. Leaders guide and support and then sit back to cheer from the sidelines."
— Simon Sinek

Micromanaging is the equivalent of sucking the life out of people at work like a vampire. I truly hope you NEVER experience this. If you have, you're nodding vigorously right now and rolling your eyes in disgust. You know exactly what I'm talking about. Not only does this demotivate people, but it has long-term, deep effects destroying self-confidence, in some cases, for the rest of people's careers.

Why have we spent so much time talking about trust? Because trust is the cornerstone of anything you will ever try to achieve as a leader. Effective delegation requires trust; it's non-negotiable.

I'm fairly sure that people who are micromanagers didn't wake up one day and say *"Gee, I think I'll grow up to be a boss who's a jerk, create anxiety by breathing down my employees' necks, and make them question every single choice they make."* Most likely not, but somewhere along the way, they either had a manager who was like this (so they learned the wrong way to lead people) and/or they have such deep rooted insecurities that they can't fathom the idea of trusting others to do good work, great work; even better work than what the manager themselves can do.

Once you've set expectations, provided clear instructions, and the team understands their mission, **get the heck out of people's way!** Let them focus on their area of genius. Letting people get to work doesn't mean you're abandoning them. It means giving them opportunities to achieve things they can be proud of. When you can't effectively delegate, due to your fears, you're robbing someone of their development. Chew on that for a bit.

You may be thinking "Ok, I get it, but it's so hard to let go. How do I actually implement?"

To remain present without hovering (and stressing your people out):

- Secure the resources and tools they need to meet their objectives.
- When they approach you with a roadblock, don't automatically solve it. Ask leading questions. If the problem is bigger than what they're equipped to handle, help them find the resources to continue.
- Establish checkpoints to keep each other informed about progress.
- Explain that you grant them the autonomy to make informed decisions. Clarify where the boundaries are, and when they should check-in with you before proceeding (e.g., spending over x dollar amount).
- Offer guidance and support their decisions. **Again — resist the urge to take the reins.** I call this 'sitting on your hands'. If you're constantly jumping in, they can't exercise their critical thinking, discernment, and problem solving skills.

- Reassure them that it's ok to make mistakes, AND follow-through with genuine support through your actions, words, and non-verbal cues.

I purposely saved this bullet point for last. Get comfortable with the fact that someone or something will eventually fail! **Failure is inevitable for learning.**

Teach your team to fail fast, get up quickly, and give themselves grace. It may be the first time your team has ever heard this. Be patient. At first, they may think you're giving them lip service and won't believe you right away. That's why owning your mistakes and showing them how to properly handle them is so important. Mistakes are part of the process. Course-correct, learn the lesson, avoid the future pitfall, and move on.

DAY 18: CHANGE MANAGEMENT

Humans are creatures of habit. We cling to our routines, the familiar, what we've learned over time and perceive to be "true".

If you have a team who is mostly excited about change, you may be fixing a broken culture who is more than happy to have you at the helm. But humans are humans. Habits are hard to change for all of us, and people don't like change. As you start diving into team objectives and see gaps, observe first, then take time to improve processes and make adjustments. Recognize the amount of change taking place or perceived "as being thrown at" them, and how to effectively manage it with your team.

You don't necessarily have to over-explain everything, but giving context builds trust and learning. Explaining 'why' is critical before you begin making even the smallest of changes. You can consider using words such as 'adjustment' or 'tweak' if it makes sense, but don't even think about starting a change without explaining why. This includes your team AND important stakeholders who may be impacted by a process either in the pre or post stages. Ask for input from your leader, peers, and team.

Your focus on building relationships will continue to play a key role in this next stage. Where you have the ability to make your team and key business partners part of the change, hear what they have to say. When possible, implement their suggestions as part of next steps. This will go a long way in building partnerships and gaining support.

To explain the "Why", try saying:

- Here's why we're adjusting that process
- After observing x and listening to the team
- I've chosen this direction because
- Leadership is prioritizing x because... ~ *Now, I caution you here that if you say anything like this for organizational-wide changes, make sure you explain who "Leadership" is, otherwise this could quickly backfire and be perceived as 'our manager is just doing what they're being told to do.'*

When people understand the "why," they're more likely to support the "what." Consider that some of the changes you're making may be final decisions, but there might be room in others for 'trial and error' and to make tweaks after a pilot period. Whatever the case is, explain it so your team understands what you're marching towards and why these strategies will help everyone get there.

DAY 19: GIVE FEEDBACK, INPUT & GUIDANCE

Giving and hearing feedback is hard, and not just because of what's said (much of which CAN actually be good and meant to help), but because it puts both giver and receiver in positions of vulnerability. When you find yourself doubting whether to say something or not, remember that clarity, when expressed with positive intent, equals respect, showing kindness for the other person. When you keep feedback silent because you're afraid of how the other person will react, you may be inadvertently doing them a disservice and taking an opportunity to grow away from them, ultimately being unkind.

Today, reflect on how your team has been exposed to feedback, how you can thoughtfully give it, and openly receive it.

- *Are they used to hearing only the bad, critical stuff?*
- *Have they only been told how great they are, but not given honest and constructive feedback?*
- *Are you unconsciously doing someone a disservice, an unkindness, by not saying what they need to hear? This includes positive and constructive input.*
- *As part of the culture you've inherited, and the one you're forming, take time to understand where everyone is at, how each person likes to receive feedback, and how they react to it.*

To build a culture of trust and growth, people need to hear balanced input. When someone is doing good things – please tell them! When they're making strides toward a goal or working hard to change their behavior, recognize their efforts.

Have you ever worked for someone who never said what they thought about you, or your work? I have. It sucks. It made my blood pressure skyrocket when they asked to meet with me (and I naturally have low blood pressure so that says it all). It taught me that I when I became a leader, I'd never do that to anyone.

Did they do it on purpose? I don't think so. They were put in a position where they didn't want to be a leader in the first place and made their displeasure well-known to their employees. **Don't be this manager.**

Don't Wait For An Annual Review

If you want to bring out the best in others, don't let small moments go unnoticed. Let me be clear – don't be fake or go praising every little thing; this is about showing gratitude. Genuinely say "thank you". Demonstrate that you're observant and present.

The same applies for underperformance. Some leaders think its merciful and benevolent to wait and have "the talk" during an annual review. Let me tell you right now – it's not, it never will be. It's a cop-out excuse because they're scared to deal with the issue. These types of leaders aren't asking for help; they're petrified to do the hard work and instead decide to ignore it, as if it will go away on its own.

Would you like your manager to wait a whole year to tell you that you're not meeting expectations at work? Of course not! If you knew, you could've had a chance to reflect, make improvements, and get better. But now you're hearing this from the person across the desk or screen, feeling like the rug was pulled out from underneath you, knowing it affected your results and now, your raise.

These conversations ARE HARD. No one becomes a manager 'just knowing' how to do this stuff. Great leaders don't do things alone. Go find HR. Yes, HR. Go talk to them, ask for help. Talk to your leader. Talk to a trusted peer manager. Role play, practice; do whatever you need to do and take that critical first step.

Diving Into Tough Feedback

What about someone whose behaviors are derailing their performance AND that of the team's? No matter the situation, good leaders provide clarity rooted in respect. No one goes into leadership because they love having uncomfortable conversations.

To grow is to change states. This requires moving from the familiar to the unknown – that's discomfort. It's how you'll develop others, and yourself in the process.

When giving feedback, use this formula; say:

- What you observed+
- Why it matters+
- What you need going forward

Here are some examples:

Example 1:
"You did a really nice job of presenting at our staff meeting today and asking for the team's input about the new

project. You stepped outside your comfort zone, and it paid off. I know it makes you uncomfortable, but it's a key skill as the project lead. The more you practice, the more confident you'll become at presenting your ideas in front of others."

Example 2:
"I noticed you've been late to the last two standups this week, and this distracts the team. It's important we all respect each other's time. Can you help me understand what happened? What prevented you from joining on time?" Pause, let them respond, listen. Then, focus on the solution. Proceed with something such as: "Thanks for letting me know about x. That said, we all need to arrive on time. Moving forward, how do you plan to arrive on time?"

Give feedback that's both direct and respectful, so the other person walks away with a clear picture of what went really well, or what needs to change.

Here are strategies you can use to prepare for a tough conversation:

- Write out what you want to say; prepare to share facts that support your observations.
- Practice in front of a mirror.
- Role play with a trusted peer manager, your leader, or HR.
- Be prepared for the best and worst reactions you could experience.
- Be ready to explain "what good looks like" with tangible, clear examples.
- Be conscious of your emotions and body language and be aware of theirs.

- Listen with as much fervor and focus as when you want to be heard.
- Stay calm; if you're at a crossroads and unsure of what to do, it's ok to take a pause and reconvene the next day.

When you make feedback a regular part of your culture—not a scary event—your team will grow to respect you and see your willingness to be fair.

Build positive intent and honesty with people, and they'll grow to understand that you're giving them feedback because you want the best for them. Not because you're out to get them or have a hidden agenda.

By practicing the sharing of balanced feedback equally with everyone on your team, they'll begin to trust that you have their back, and they'll have yours.

What If I'm The One Who Messed Up? What Should I Do If Something Goes Sideways?

Honesty IS the best policy. We ALL make mistakes, most times unintentionally, because we didn't understand the full scope of an issue or its impact. Project failures, a conversation that went poorly, missing deadlines, failing to plan properly…it happens to the best of leaders.

When you make a mistake, don't try to hide it or cover it up. That's the worst thing you can do. While you may want to fix it yourself as quickly as possible, I recommend the exact opposite.

In our anxiety to fix a problem we think will make our leader furious (our mind will invent a TON of negative scenarios under pressure), we could make things go from bad to worse in a heartbeat.

Stop and think – do you really know how to solve it? If you're not 100% sure, find your leader and ask for help. If they're not around, find another leader. Share what happened, your suggestion, then listen and follow the next best step. Take responsibility. Listen to what they have to say. I'm dead serious; now isn't the time to deflect or blame. That will backfire. Just focus on the solution.

Once things have settled down, you can circle back with your leader. Consider your apology. Calmly explain the context. If what occurred was outside of your control, you'll likely be frustrated and want to 'defend' yourself.

Use your emotional intelligence; be open to learning and discussing the facts from beginning to end so that you can understand your leader's perspective. Remain open to their coaching; ask questions about what you can do differently and show that you've learned a valuable lesson. Self-reflect and give yourself grace. And then, move on. Go for a run, watch a show, get ice cream, read a book. Things always look better in the morning.

DAY 20: CONFLICT 101

There's no getting around it – just hearing the word 'conflict' evokes discomfort. If left to our instincts, humans avoid conflict like the plague, especially when it comes to tough situations at work. Just because you're a manager, doesn't mean you get fairy dust sprinkled on you, and now suddenly love managing conflict.

Every person is different; some personalities are more open to conflict and handle it straight on, while others are more cautious and thoughtful. Neither is right or wrong, it's simply who we are, and both approaches have their place.

It's ok to recognize that even though we're managers, we're human and aren't excited about dealing with conflict. **What IS critical is that we understand how to effectively take action, so we can ultimately build stronger, healthier teams.** Let's acknowledge the role of healthy conflict, learn how to respond (not react), and practice staying curious during tension.

Isn't Conflict the Enemy?

Initially, your instinct might be to avoid conflict to "keep the peace." But the truth is: conflict is inevitable. When handled properly, it can build trust, drive innovation, and strengthen relationships. Think of conflict like fire: unmanaged, it burns down trust. When well-managed, it can be the spark for clarity, progress, and growth.

What Types of Conflict Will I Face?

Conflicts are sticky. They come in all shapes and sizes. From lively team discussions to approve a final product design, an impromptu call from an upset service technician who's mad about another mechanic not returning tools they borrowed, a process change, an employee's tardiness, a company benefit you have nothing to do with, something you didn't realize you said, did, or didn't do, heated contract negotiations, addressing underperformance, improper behaviors, team members bringing their personal problems into work, lack of follow-through… You get the idea – there's more than 31 flavors to choose from, and you can't predict how or when it's going to show up.

Whether it's a planned tough conversation, or a surprise *"do you have 5 minutes to talk, I'm really upset"* visit (as you're running out the door to pick up your kids at 4pm on a Friday), let's talk about how to best prepare. I'll give you tools and scripts, but you've got to understand this is one of those things you have to face with courage.

Will you be nervous? Yes. Will your stomach churn? Potentially. Will you have situations happening right in front of you and think *"Oh my gosh, I have no clue what to say next."* You bet.

Trust me, you're not the first and you won't be the last. The more conflicts you face, the more skilled you'll grow in applying your emotional intelligence to navigate all sorts of sticky situations. Keep seeking support; talk to your manager, a trusted peer, or HR to replay what's already happened, or help you prep for an upcoming conversation.

Conflict Is So Complex, What *Can* I Do?

Stay curious, not combative. Aim to listen.

Conflict escalates when people feel dismissed, attacked, or unheard. As a leader, your job is to stay calm, grounded, and curious, ESPECIALLY when emotions run high. During times of unexpected conflict, the most powerful tool you have is this question:

"Can you help me understand …?"

- What's behind that perspective?
- Why you're saying this?
- What leads you to believe this?

Here's a 4-Step Conflict Framework to guide conflict conversations:

1. **Pause & Breathe:** Take at least 2 deep breaths. This will give your brain space to respond, not react.
2. **Acknowledge Emotion:** "This is frustrating, I hear you, let's figure this out."
3. **Ask & Listen:** Use open-ended questions like, *"What happened?, What feels unresolved for you?, What could be the best next step?"*
4. **Agree on Next Steps:** Even if you don't know have the end-solution right now, make it clear to define what the next best step will be. You may or may not be directly involved in that action, but don't leave the conversation without clarifying expectations and timelines. Summarize to help everyone stay on track.

This approach defuses tension and shows you're listening with positive intent, to learn — not win. **Your goal here** isn't to 'be right'. Your mission is to unravel and calm emotions, bring facts forward, and arrive at resolution.

Here are words to use in tense moments: *"It sounds like we're seeing things differently, and I want to understand your point of view. Let's talk through what's important to both of us and see where we can find common ground."*

If emotions are escalating, it's best to listen, wait for a few moments, and calmly suggest you take a pause and revisit the next day.

You could say: *"I can see this means a lot to you. I respect you and want to work through this with you. For us both to be in a good position to do that, let's pause our conversation for now, and come back to it tomorrow."*

If the other person continues, and doesn't want to leave or stop talking, give them a few moments, but don't allow them to spiral. You're in control. You don't need to yell or raise your voice. If they raise theirs, lower yours. Calmly, firmly, and respectfully, repeat what you said, and make it clear that you're not to going to discuss this anymore today.

While I hope it never comes to this, if their response and emotions are too overwhelming, be ready to ask the person to go home for the day and walk them out. **If they're not respecting you, the team, or your workplace, and you don't feel emotionally or physically safe, they need to leave ASAP.** Find back-up support from HR or another manager if you need it.

It's better to take a breath and seek advice before saying something you or the other person will regret. While you can go back to apologize, *you can never take back how you made someone feel – regardless of who is in the 'right'.*

"Planned Conflict" Addressing Underperformance

After just a couple weeks on the job, you're starting to get reports that a team member isn't pulling their weight. Maybe you need to have a conversation, but it's so hard; you're still getting to know the basics – how can you call someone in to make judgments about their performance? Isn't it too soon?

Every situation is different. It comes down to facts. If you have concrete examples, emails, and unsolicited feedback from peers, managers or customers, it's time to have a conversation.

First, assume positive intent. Gather facts; how long has this been happening, who's observed it, are there supporting outcomes…?

What do you know about this person so far? Talents, personality, potential triggers…?

Going into these conversations, we're so anxious about the prep; the reason for scheduling it, how to start, thinking the worst about how they'll react… that we forget to define: *What's the outcome I'm looking for?* **It's like we packed the car for a big road trip, filled up with gas, got snacks, threw the luggage in and starting driving - but have no idea where we're actually going.**

What do you REALLY know?

I once worked with a high performer who was veering off track. It was unusual and it worried me. When speaking with them *(not to them)*, it turned out their mother was critically ill. They were facing whether to admit her into a nursing home or bring her home with them. They were scared to tell anyone. We got them connected with HR, who helped them work through a temporary leave and provided supporting resources. The team was more than willing to create a plan to divide and conquer while they were away.

Don't predisposition the conversation; don't assume you know the cause. Go one step at a time and seek to understand. You could start with:

"Hi [Name], thank you for meeting with me. I'd like to get your perspective on [name the process/challenge]. When working on [Task X], the outcomes haven't consistently met the high standards our customers expect (explain why with examples and facts). Could you help me understand what you're seeing from your side?"

Then zip it and listen. Watch for verbal and non-verbal cues. If their response confirms a performance, learning, or skill gap, proceed with something like this:

"I understand what you're describing about the process changes and why it's making it more challenging for you to meet our customer's expectations. Here's what [I/the team/customers] have observed [show examples, and why it's not working] when you do x. Here's what good looks like [show an example of good email communication, process flow, etc.]. Let's outline a plan on how to achieve results that match the objective; what are your suggestions?" After, say *"let's get a weekly check-in on our calendars to make sure things are working the way we expect."*

Be sure to gather feedback and tell them how they're progressing when you meet.

What if I sense there's a personal challenge?

While you need to be careful of asking personal questions, you may get a sense that there's something more. You could open the door for them to share what they're comfortable with, and let them know you're there to be a resource:

- *"I've noticed you seem a little off lately, and I wanted to check in. Is everything okay?"*
- *"How's your workload feeling right now? Is there anything we could adjust to make things more manageable for you?"*
- *"Are there any resources the company offers that you'd be interested in learning about?"* (This points them toward Employee Assistance Programs or other benefits without being intrusive.)

Let them share what they're comfortable with, but don't push. Say *"you don't need to answer anything you don't want to, I just want to make sure you're ok, and I'm here to help if you need me."* Give them information to seek out HR or other resources as appropriate.

Close the dialogue on a positive note:

"Thank you for speaking with me today. I appreciate your honesty. Now that we have a plan to proceed with x, and check-in weekly on Wednesdays, this will give you the tools to stay on track and I'll have better insights into the process too so I can better coach you and our team. If you have any questions prior to our next check-in, please reach out."

DAY 21: WEEKLY REFLECTION

This week you dug really deep. Seriously. Like preparing for an exam or a competition, you're doing exactly what it takes to shape critical parts of not just your team's culture, but who you are as their leader. You're shaping your own core values; values you'll teach by example.

Communicating expectations is how leaders set the stage for accountability, alignment, and autonomy. Growth conversations can bring discomfort but climbing that hill means getting others to a better place – why good leaders accept the challenge. Jot down your thoughts for this week:

Reflect

- *Did I clearly communicate expectations?*
- *What went well in feedback conversations?*
- *Where might I need to clarify or follow up?*

✓ Takeaway for Week 3:

You're creating clarity. You're opening space for two-way feedback. You're leading with transparency and your team is starting to trust the direction you're setting. Lean into these behaviors and trust that you're doing the right things to move forward.

WEEK 4
Grow Into Your Leadership Style

DAY 22: DEVELOP YOUR LEADERSHIP BRAND

What Is a Leadership Brand?

Your leadership brand is the combination of the actions, values, and behaviors that define how others experience you as a leader.

Your brand isn't synonymous with being a perfect leader — it's about being intentional, consistent, and caring for the well-being of those you lead.

Consider…

"When people talk about me as a leader, what do I want them to think, say, and feel?"

Start With Your Strengths

Every great leader builds their style around what they naturally do well. Look back at the last 3 weeks.

Reflect on your best days or moments — what patterns show up? Where have you naturally excelled?

Ask Yourself:

- *What conversations felt the most intuitive to me?*
- *What feedback have I received (formal or informal)?*
- *When did I feel most confident?*

Here's a list of leadership strengths to consider:

- Empathy and active listening
- Staying calm and focused in urgent situations
- Decision-making under pressure
- Coaching others to solve problems
- Creating psychological safety
- Strong organizational skills
- Leading with curiosity
- Encouraging collaboration
- Coaching for professional development
- Displaying positive intent
- Facilitating a tough conversation
- Being a sounding board for your manager
- Addressing underperformance respectfully
- Fostering team brainstorming to develop their own suggestions for improvement

> ### TAKE ACTION
>
> **Revisit your Leadership Mission Statement from Days 1 and 4.** I frequently and purposely repeat this throughout the book because your Leadership Statement will keep evolving as you grow. It's your personal map, keeping you in check and on the right track.
>
> Another way to think about your Leadership Brand is to complete this sentence:
> *"I am the kind of leader who ___, ___, and ___."*
>
> Choose 3 strengths you want to be known for. Think of a time you used each strength to lead meaningfully; when you felt that genuine, positive impact was received by the other person.
>
> **Examples:**
> - *"I am the kind of leader who listens deeply, sets clear priorities, and develops others."*
> - *"I am the kind of leader who leads with curiosity, makes brave decisions, and learns from feedback."*

Revisit your Leadership Brand and Mission Statement often. Not necessarily because it needs changing, but because when you read it repeatedly, you let it ground you, you bring yourself back to center. This is your compass, motivating you to keep going when you're proud of your actions and to be an alert when you stray off course.

Don't be afraid to own your strengths. Name them and be proud—they're your talents, the foundation of your leadership. You CAN be a humble leader and simultaneously know what you're good at.

You just need to make sure that your self-awareness is tuned in to both sides of the coin—your strengths and your growth edges.

DAY 23: RECOGNIZE YOUR GROWTH EDGES

Growth requires honesty. What's been the hardest part about being a leader so far? It's ok to be honest with yourself. No one knows you better than you. Being a coach, guide, facilitator, and even a referee some days – it's hard. Let's be real. Leadership is incredibly rewarding; there are days when you're flying so high, no amount of challenges can bring you down. But there will also be days that mentally drain you to the point of wishing you hadn't gotten out of bed. If people were consistent, if change was nonexistent, if needs didn't change…you get the picture. Meaningful leadership at any level takes time, patience, and perseverance. Show up, one day at a time. And on those really TOUGH days, sometimes it's just about conquering one hour at a time.

What Are "Growth Edges"?

Your growth edges are the points where your current skills, mindset, and comfort zone are being stretched.

They're not just weaknesses — they're invitations to level up. Gaining this self-awareness doesn't mean that we should try to conquer all our weaknesses, but it opens our eyes to realize we may need to find extra resources and support to compensate for the areas that don't come naturally.

Ask Yourself:

"What part of leadership feels hardest right now — and what might that be teaching me?"

Here's Some Common Growth Edges for New Managers (and Experienced Ones Too)

- Fear of delegating so instead, you do it all yourself
- Giving feedback in real time
- Avoiding difficult conversations or sugarcoating the message (therefore losing its intent)
- Micromanaging: making constant decisions for others because you're afraid the output will be less than ideal
- Struggling with staying steady and calm under pressure, when things don't go as planned
- Feeling like you constantly need to explain yourself, justify your expertise, or why you're in this role
- Getting caught in 'analysis paralysis' when making decisions...

Did any one of these make you tense up? Congrats on being normal! Yes, you're a fully living and breathing human being who's growing. Growth simply can't happen without discomfort. When you work to understand how these tensions hold you back, that's a sign you're focused on getting better and becoming the kind of impactful leader people talk about at the dinner table, in a good way.

You're at the intersection of discomfort and development. Right where growth happens. Your goal is to identify the areas where you feel uneasiness, resistance, and uncertainty — and see them as powerful opportunities for growth. But let me be clear – it's **NOT to put yourself down.** Try this prompt to name a current growth edge for you:

"I notice I get stuck or uncomfortable when ____. *I think this is an opportunity to grow in* ____.*"*

Example:

"I notice I get stuck when I have to give feedback to high performers. I think this is an opportunity to grow in courageous communication."

Other helpful prompts include:

- *What am I avoiding? What gets moved to last place?*
- *What feedback triggered discomfort in me?*
- *When did I feel unsure or disconnected?*

Take Action
Write down one growth edge and commit to taking a small step toward it this week. Tell a mentor, coach, or peer for support and accountability.

Challenge yourself to take just one growth edge and observe yourself in the coming weeks. Recognize it when it shows up. At first, you don't need to solve or fix it. Get comfortable identifying it and defining what brought it on, what's happening around you, and how others are reacting.

As you begin to understand when and how this growth edge shows up, you'll be better equipped to think before speaking or taking action. Replay these scenarios in your mind. Come up alternatives on how to respond. In time, while butterflies may still be present, your courage muscle will get stronger and help you take the next best step.

You're not expected to be perfect—just present and growing. There are times when assessing one's own triggers as a leader, will be more impactful for you than the "act" of solving the situation at hand. Practice turns into progress. You'll fine-tune your self-awareness, giving yourself the time and space to make the right calls, especially when it comes to hard choices outside your comfort zone.

DAY 24: DEFINE HEALTHY BOUNDARIES

Great leaders want to connect with their teams, be open, and available. That said, being a leader doesn't mean being available 24/7 or saying yes to everything. Being 'open' doesn't mean telling everyone intimate details about your personal life and innermost thoughts.

Setting clear, healthy boundaries from the start protects your energy, models respect and enables you to sustainably lead your team. You're also teaching them to do the same! This doesn't mean you can't form genuine relationships. You can simultaneously have healthy boundaries AND form strong bonds. You just need to understand where the balance lies.

Why Do Boundaries Matter?

As a new manager, it's tempting to be available 24/7, say "yes" to everything, or constantly put others' needs above your own. But this leads to burnout — and confusion about what's acceptable and what's not.

Boundaries aren't barriers; they provide clarity and the strength to sustain your well-being. They help your team understand how to work with you effectively and show that self-respect and mutual respect go hand in hand.

Where Do You Need Boundaries?

These may differ with circumstances, but here are some areas to consider:
- **Time:** When are you making yourself available?
- **Communication:** What's your preferred method for others to reach out and vice versa? How are you defining "urgent" vs what can wait?
- **Workload:** Are you taking on too much to "prove yourself"?
- **Personal values:** Are you honoring your own capacity and limits? Your family and friend time?

Consider:

- When do you need uninterrupted 'focus' time?
- How do you recharge?
- What practices aren't sustainable long-term?

Healthy boundaries = long-term sustainability.

You've got to think about your boundaries, set them, and share them. Your team can't read your mind!

Here are some example statements you can use to clarify healthy boundaries:

- I'm available for questions between 9am–5pm. If it's urgent after hours, for example an unexpected product outage, please send a text asap!
- I block two hours on my calendar each week for deep work so I can stay focused on priorities.
- It's important to me that we disconnect fully on weekends so we can return refreshed (depending on the nature of your work, shifts, etc.).

- If we're outside our staff meeting, or regular 1:1 and you need to touch base, I have 2-3pm blocked on my calendar Mondays and Thursdays for questions.

If it's hard for you to shape some of these, think of at least one boundary that if used consistently, will help you show up more effectively.

As you get to know your team, some people may feel more open to sharing personal stories and situations with you. While you want to be empathetic, listen with intent, and have fun, be aware if situations start to go outside of normal boundaries. An employee telling you deeply intimate life details that make you uncomfortable or talking to you like their therapist isn't a recipe for success, for either of you. If you're in a situation like this, reach out to your leader, a trusted peer, or HR ASAP for guidance on how to steer the situation kindly and professionally.

DAY 25: SEEK LEADERSHIP FEEDBACK

Feedback Is a Mirror, Not a Final Verdict

Everyone I know hates the word 'feedback'. Do you? Be honest! No matter how many times I talk about balance, it's almost impossible to crack the code because we're conditioned to equate feedback with criticism. Criticism hurts. It makes us feel flawed and inadequate. Deep down, most humans are triggered by feedback. But feedback – let's call it "input", is how we learn what's working and what may need adjusting.

It's normal to feel uncomfortable about receiving and giving input to others. When you invite and receive suggestions with openness, you show your team that growth and humility are at your leadership core. Because people are used to negative input, balanced feedback will take time for your team to understand, especially if they've been conditioned to 'wait for the other shoe to drop' in the past.

Don't wait for a formal review to ask.

Want to grow faster? Ask your team, peers, or your manager: *"I'm still learning in this role, and I'd love to know, what's one thing I could do more of—or less of—to be a better leader for you and our team?"*

Asked differently, *"What's one thing I can Start, Stop, or Continue doing to support you better?"*

Keep it short and open-ended, with low stakes. When you ask for input in person, be aware of your tone and keep your body language open. Model humility. Take notes. Thank them. This builds culture and self-awareness.

Getting Over the Fear

Trust me — you'll get input — solicited and unsolicited. In your first weeks, if you receive unsolicited feedback that feels 'judgy' and you're unsure how to respond, avoid defending yourself, making up a solution, or justifying.

The best way to respond is to say, "thank you". It's as simple as that and requires nothing more: *"Thanks for sharing this with me. I'm learning and will take the time to reflect on what you've shared with me."*

You don't have to fix everything overnight. You can't! Don't go into a rant explaining why they don't understand your position. Don't spiral and doubt whether you're right for the role. Definitely don't do this!

You thank them, reflect, and decide what you can act on. You can always follow up with them later. Doing anything else will bring emotion into the conversation that won't help either of you succeed.

How Do I Take the "Ick" Out of Feedback?

By making it part of your culture. People are scared of any kind of input because we automatically assume the worst– it's our fight or flight instinct. When you make it a point to give balanced input on a regular basis – and ask for it regularly, in time, it'll become less weird, and part of your team's encouraging culture.

How to Normalize Feedback

- Ask for input during 1:1s (with reports, peers, and manager) and staff meetings
- Share what you're working to improve or compensate for
- Show appreciation: "Thanks for sharing that — it helps me grow and lead better for our team."

Whatever you call it – feedback, input, suggestions, or comments – don't let good work OR underperformance go unnoticed. When your team knows you and their peers come from a place of positive intent, you'll create a culture where honesty and development are the norm, not a rarity.

DAY 26: LEAD WITH AUTHENTICITY

Don't try to be the leader others think you "should" be—be the leader your team needs. Be true to yourself.

Authentic leadership isn't having all the answers, sharing everything, or knowing exactly what to say and do. An authentic leader has the courage to act with ethics, curiosity, and vulnerability. They consistently demonstrate what matters to them and their team by being accountable and clear in their actions.

People don't follow titles—they follow authenticity. Actions that back up your words solidify trust. You'll attract allies who will show up to help you succeed and guide you through tough times.

Authentic leaders ask:

- *Am I leading from my values?*
- *Do my actions match my intentions?*
- *How can I show up more fully as myself?*

Demonstrate real leadership by:

- Admitting when you don't know something
- Sharing what you're learning
- Connecting people to each other as resources
- Asking questions instead of proving knowledge
- Aligning your choices with your values
- Staying grounded in difficult moments

Check-In on Team Engagement

Communication is a two-way street. It's not enough to talk—how's your message actually landing?

We have two ears and one mouth for a reason. The more we listen, the more we learn. Successful teams are built by thoughtful leaders who understand the power of listening intently. That's engagement.

Leaders who create a space where others feel safe to ask questions AND give their opinion, open the doors to collaboration, creativity, and inclusion. This starts by asking questions with positive intent and genuine curiosity:

- *How are you? What's been going well for you lately?*
- *What's felt frustrating or unclear?*
- *If you had the means to solve any problem here, what would that be?*

Keep it conversational. Ask, and then zip it! Listen more than you speak. Thank them for their honesty. Using questions like these will help you find missed opportunities and solve more problems than you ever imagined.

DAY 27: CELEBRATE WINS & PROGRESS (THEIRS + YOURS)

Look at how far you and your team have come in just 4 weeks! Can you believe it?

No, I'm not naïve; I know you haven't solved every problem that's been handed to you, and there are still big challenges ahead.

Have pride in how far you've come! You're moving mountains; that's what you're doing.

Why Celebration Matters

Big wins are great — but so are the quieter victories:

- A team member stepped up with initiative,
- A tough conversation you navigated with care,
- A process that's working more smoothly,
- A behavior shift that reflects growth,
- A positive culture shift that your team embraced…

The point is always progress. Momentum builds motivation.

Simple Ways to Celebrate & Acknowledge Wins

Maybe you have the budget to bring in lunch or a snack for the team, maybe you don't. Can you bake some cookies or do something simple? While big perks are awesome, and you should implement them when you can, there's no replacement for genuine, everyday ways to recognize wins:

- Acknowledge someone in a meeting
- Send a quick thank you or kudos email (copy their manager if they don't report to you!)
- Drop a hand-written note on their desk with a treat or piece of candy
- Share a "win of the week" on a virtual channel, during a 1:1, or make it a regular part of your staff meeting
- Reflect on 3 things you're proud of that the team accomplished this month
- Encourage your team to give each other shoutouts

When gratitude is specific, timely, and genuine, people will remember how you made them feel, and what they can accomplish together as a team.

DAY 28: WEEKLY REFLECTION

You've successfully navigated a period of rapid growth. You're pushing yourself every day, many times leaving your comfort zone. You're mentally exhausted but every ounce of your effort is worth it — even when you can't see results right away. If no one else has told you lately, I'm telling you. Now it's up to you to believe it.

Working your tail off, visibly, and most times quietly, pays off. Every challenge you face is like a workout for your leadership skills, making them stronger over time.

Pause to reflect on your growth and intentions for the coming days. These Weekly Reflections are easy to skim over. It's tempting to keep pushing forward, mainly because you've got too much on your plate and have too many deadlines to meet. Trust me. Great leaders understand that reflection fuels awareness, learning, and purpose.

It doesn't matter how long you've been a leader. Take a walk, sit outside, go get yourself a coffee. Purposely taking that time alone to review what you've experienced, deepens your development. Don't laugh; I'm serious. It's not fluffy HR stuff. You're connecting the dots — not just between random meetings, but between specific events, what you learned, and who you're becoming.

This week was all about:
- Defining your boundaries
- Asking for and reflecting on feedback
- Exploring your authentic leadership style

- Tuning into your team's level of engagement
- Celebrating individual and team wins

REFLECT

- *What do I know now about myself as a leader?*
- *Where am I most proud of my growth?*
- *What still feels hard—but most importantly, what am I learning from it?*
- *How will I continue investing in my leadership journey?*

This is the work that matters—and you're doing it.

✓ **Takeaway for Week 4:**

You're not just managing—you're leading. You're on the path to becoming the kind of leader people remember for the right reasons.

WEEK 5

Refocus & Realign for Self-Motivation

DAY 29: FINISH STRONG & PREPARE FOR WHAT'S NEXT

You've made it through your first month as a new manager—congratulations! You've shown up consistently for over 4 weeks. You've asked hard questions, reflected deeply, connected authentically, and made progress, recognizing that growth doesn't happen in a straight line. Before rushing into what's next, take a moment to honor what this means. You're not the same person you were when you started on this path.

> ### Reflect
>
> - *What surprised me the most about leading this team and becoming their manager?*
> - *What were my biggest wins this month?*
> - *What mindsets, habits, or pre-conceived notions shifted the most for me?*
> - *What mistakes or mis-steps taught me something important?*
> - *What systems or habits helped me stay grounded?*
> - *What feedback did I receive—and how am I growing from it?*
> - *What am I most proud of?*

Capture Your Top 5 Leadership Lessons:

1. ────────────────────────
2. ────────────────────────
3. ────────────────────────
4. ────────────────────────
5. ────────────────────────

REFLECT

Consider this question:

- *If I could go back and give my "Day 1 self" one piece of advice, what would it be?*

Your answer is a powerful tool for your own growth and for the future leaders you'll be developing. Leadership is about life-long learning; trying, failing, succeeding, adjusting, and persevering—so that we ultimately become the best orchestrators we can be for our teams and others around us.

Make no mistake; you're doing this! You're growing every single step of the way. **Don't let anyone say or make you feel otherwise — especially YOU.**

That's right, you heard me. Most of the time, you'll be your worst critic. That pesky, annoying, powerful visitor called 'Impostor Syndrome,' who loves to lurk in the shadows, will knock at your door, repeatedly and without warning. You don't have time or energy to waste on Impostor

Syndrome. Your energy is simply too precious and valuable. It has no right to invade your space.

When it starts creeping in, and it will, kick it the hell out. If you're struggling, ask for help. Turn to good mentors, friends, and trusted sources—these are your allies; the ones who'll remind you of your purpose and talents when you need it most. And you'll be a source of support to them.

They'll show up for you, yet always know this: *you are responsible for motivating yourself.* Whether through continued education, conferences, reading, podcasts, peer industry groups...always keep yourself engaged.

You were placed in this role because you're the person who's meant to move this mountain; to propel your team, values, and mission forward.

DAY 30: YOUR 60 & 90-DAY ROADMAP

Why a Roadmap?

You've done the hard work focusing your efforts and building momentum, but we can't stop there. Now it's time to transform that momentum into a sustainable plan. This roadmap will help you stay aligned with your goals and set clarity for yourself in your next phase.

Studies have shown that people who write down their goals and plans are more likely to achieve them, compared to those who don't.

Which group are you in?

In the coming months you'll continue practicing servant leadership by *deepening trust, increasing impact,* and *evolving your leadership style* with intention.

Your 60-Day Goals: Stabilize & Strengthen

Focus on:

- Deepening 1:1s and coaching your team
- Strengthening relationships with cross-functional partners, internal, and external stakeholders
- Creating clarity around processes, ownership, and priorities
- Following up on feedback and sharing progress
- Building the partnership with your leader

Think About:

- *Where does my team still need clarity or support?*
- *What processes or tools are slowing us down?*
- *Where can I empower team members more?*

TAKE ACTION
Write a short letter to yourself with a couple of bullet points that starts with: *"Dear Future Me, here's what I want to remember about this experience..."* Tuck it inside your notes and revisit in 60 days.

Your 90-Day + Goals: Strategize & Scale

This phase is about setting your team up for long-term success.

Shift to:

- **Elevating your leadership brand** with visibility and influence
- **Strategic thinking:** how does your team fit into the broader, big picture of company goals?
- Deeper dives into **systems and processes**
- **Mentoring** existing and future leaders on your team

Think About:

- *How does our work connect to the larger mission?*
- *What changes could increase our impact or efficiency?*
- *How am I shaping the culture I want to be part of?*
- *What are my team's aspirations? Are there high-performers seeking more opportunities?*

Create Your Personalized 60/90-Day and Beyond Plans

Final Challenge:

Reflect on your 60, 90-Day and beyond growth areas. Fill in the roadmap with your personal goals. Share it with your manager, mentor, or HR. Ask them to be allies and support your continued growth.

60-Day Focus Areas:

1. ───────────────────────
2. ───────────────────────
3. ───────────────────────

90-Day Focus Areas:

1. ───────────────────────
2. ───────────────────────
3. ───────────────────────

Long-Term 'Beyond' Focus Areas:

1. ───────────────────────
2. ───────────────────────
3. ───────────────────────

Sample 60/90-Day Roadmap

Area	60-Day Goal	90-Day Goal
Team	Build trust, deepen 1:1s	Align on team goals + outcomes
Self-Leadership	Reflect & seek feedback	Share leadership vision more confidently
Strategy	Understand priorities	Improve 1 process or practice
Culture	Model values, celebrate wins	Launch one team engagement habit

Your 60/90—Day Roadmap

Area	60—Day Goal	90—Day Goal
Area 1		
Area 2		
Area 3		
Area 4		

Your Long-Term 'Beyond' Roadmap

Area	Long-Term & Beyond Goals
Area 1	
Area 2	
Area 3	
Area 4	

BONUS CHAPTER: BUILD YOUR TEAM WITH INTENTION

There's a critical topic you can't afford to overlook: how to hire top-notch talent.

Hiring Isn't Just HR's Job

Hiring top talent isn't just an HR function—it's one of your most important responsibilities as a manager. The people you bring in will shape your culture, performance, and ultimately, your success.

HR or recruiters may screen résumés, schedule interviews, or manage logistics, but they're not building your team—you are. Even if hiring is outsourced, no one knows the skills, behaviors, and culture you need better than you. *Hiring IS your responsibility.*

Think of recruiters as partners: they facilitate the process, but it's your job to communicate requirements clearly, engage in the interviews, and make the final decision. Whether it's internal HR or an external firm, a recruiter can't read your mind or assess the necessary skills required for the role. If you're acting as both manager and recruiter, these principles become even more critical.

Hiring with a Strategy, Not Hope

You wouldn't rely on "hope" to hit organizational goals—you'd set targets, allocate resources, and execute a plan. Hiring deserves the same intentionality. Hope doesn't assemble dream teams.

Start with a **strategy session** to define:

- **Position Requirements:** education, industry experience, technical skills, desired behaviors.
- **Scope:** target start date, job description, reporting structure, cross-functional partners, work location.
- **Sourcing Strategy:** where and how to find candidates, equivalent job titles, job boards, networks, and your updates cadence with the recruiter.
- **Compensation & Benefits:** salary, bonus, equity, time off, health and wellness.
- **Interview Process:** format, interview team, evaluation criteria, decision-making steps.

Hire for Culture; You Can't Afford to Settle

While a candidate's technical abilities are essential, don't let technical 'superstardom' overshadow essentials like engagement and collaboration. You've invested too much in building a positive team culture to hire someone who looks like an A+ player on paper but shows up as an arrogant jerk nobody wants to be near.

This is especially tough when roles are left vacated for a long time. These situations will test every ounce of resilience you've got. Desperate to find a replacement, new leaders can easily fall into the trap of settling by telling themselves *"I can help this person change"* or *"it's better to have a body than nobody"*.

Sooner or later leaders end up regretting these decisions. And yes, even good leaders make hiring mistakes. If they're brave enough, they'll resolve quickly; they'll have a tough conversation ASAP, partner with HR to follow the right process, and respectfully part ways if the situation can't be resolved. Avoiding the issue creates a terrible situation—for you, your team, your company, and the hire themselves.

This is known as hiring for a good "culture fit". While this expression is well-intended, we can do so much better. Instead of asking yourself *"Is this candidate a good culture fit?"* swap that for *"What will this candidate "**add**" to our culture? How will their talents and abilities make us stronger?"* Hire for High-Performance Culture; never lower the bar on your cultural expectations.

High-Performance Culture (HPC) means daily behaviors align with company values. Signs of HPC include:

- Integrity expressed through kindness and professionalism.
- Feedback delivered candidly, with positive intent.
- No tolerance for gossip.
- Team success prioritized over individual wins.
- High say/do ratio of accountability—especially when failures occur.
- Urgency and effort directed toward helping teammates, customers, and stakeholders.

Walk Through the Candidate Experience

Before jumping to schedule interviews, put yourself in the candidate's shoes. **Design the process from the candidate's perspective!** Does a first-round panel with five interviewers make sense? Often not. Create a process that ensures you can assess necessary skills and behaviors without overwhelming them.

Remember: Candidate experience is culture in action. Candidates make judgments through each interaction, your leadership style, employee engagement, and expectations. These are the deciding factors a candidate will use to accept or decline your offer. Be responsive. Ghosting damages you and your company's reputation.

Prepare for the Interview

Before kicking off interviews, decide:

- Format by interview stage (phone, virtual, panel, or in-person).
- Which technical and behavioral competencies to evaluate.
- Who participates and who simply needs updates.
- Where to include team members.
- How to gather interview feedback and take notes.
- Whether existing templates or tools are available.

Ask the "Right" Questions

It's perfectly normal to have jitters when interviewing for the first time. First-time interviewers often worry more about what not to ask. And rightfully so— at the time of this writing, laws like the U.S. Equal Employment Opportunity Act (and similar global standards) prohibit questions about:

- Age, race, ethnicity, gender, sexual orientation, and religion;

- Country of origin, marital or family status, disability, pregnancy;
- Veteran or military status;
- Salary history (varies by state);
- Health conditions and
- Language (unless directly relevant). For example, instead of saying: "*Are you a native English speaker?*" ask: "*What languages do you speak fluently?*" if the role requires multi-language fluency.

Assess for Culture Add

Great interviewees don't always make great hires. The best way to learn what a candidate can add to your culture is to ask questions that give you insights about the depth of their engagement and commitment.

To gauge real impact, focus on three areas:

1. High-Performing Effort
2. Delivering Top Results
3. Tenacity

Your company may have already developed an effective format for evaluating talent that includes behavioral interview questions or other specific evaluations. Even when there is already a process in place, you can evaluate the responses a candidate provides by looking for these three factors.

There's an endless amount of questions you could ask in an interview, but let me assure you, it's not about how many questions you can ask in an hour. It's about the quality of questions and responses that help you assess what you need, sometimes in a limited amount of time.

Remember to be consistent in the questions you ask each candidate; good leaders ensure that an equitable and honorable interview process is followed.

To assess for 'culture-add' and high-performance, use the following questions to guide your conversation:

For High-Performing Effort – *In your last three roles, what accomplishments made you most proud? What skills or behaviors made that possible?*

For Delivering Top Results – *Tell me about your top results in the last three roles. How did you go above expectations? How was success measured?*

For Tenacity – *Describe three times in your last three roles when things didn't go as planned and you faced real setbacks. What happened, and how did you respond?*

This framework will give you a chance to learn critical details; where the candidate went "above and beyond", what their motivations are, what kind of feedback they've received, how they overcome challenges, and more. Keep interviews consistent and take notes. It's not about quantity of questions, but the quality and depth of insight they reveal.

Spotting Potential Red Flags

With experience, you'll start to notice subtle cues that matter. When starting out, invite a peer leader or HR partner to join and compare notes afterwards. Hiring comes with risks. You'll make excellent hires in your career, and you'll make mistakes too – we all do – we learn and get better each time.

Here are some clues to watch for:

- How candidates engage with everyone - from the receptionist to executives.
- Concerning language.
- Tone of voice, body language, and presence; are they 100% invested and engaged?
- How they talk about their prior work, past managers, teams, and responsibilities, team, and manager...
- How can you tell they want to join your team?

> ### INSIGHT TIP:
>
> *What do I mean by "concerning language"? Swearing and foul language is not a good sign; if a candidate speaks to you in an interview like that, how will they address a customer, teammate, or you as their manager?*
>
> *Watch especially for embedded, negative language that has nothing to do with swearing – and might be said so fast it's hard to catch.*
>
> *For example, I once interviewed a candidate for a senior manager role, who referred to their past team as a group of 'leeches'. I don't care how terrible your last job was, that's no way to talk about people. Needless to say, they were not the culture add we were looking for.*
>
> *Actively listen to responses, phrases, and words that align with your culture and values. Never settle!*

THE FINAL DECISION

At the final stage of evaluating candidates, ensure that your decision-making process reflects fairness and balance.

- Gather structured feedback from interviewers; include them in the discussion.
- Involve HR early.
- Discuss pros, cons, and cultural impact.

When you're ready to extend an offer, call the candidate yourself. **Don't skip this step or delegate it to HR or an automated system.** Nothing replaces hearing the offer come directly from the candidate's future leader. That single phone call often makes the difference between acceptance and decline.

Follow-Up and Follow Through, Especially With No

Rejection is tough—but silence is worse. If you've ever been ghosted by a recruiter or manager, you know the feeling of frustration. Respect candidates' time and effort by closing the loop, even with a "no."

It's a fact that today's workloads can be absolutely staggering. Many times lack of response to candidates is because managers and HR teams are overwhelmed and overworked. That said, find ways to be an upstanding leader; extend respect to all, including candidates you don't hire.

If you're overwhelmed, collaborate with your recruiter on how to streamline communication methods.

A respectful decline today may open the door for a different circumstance tomorrow. Remember: Every interaction leaves an impression—make it a positive one.

FINAL THOUGHTS: YOU DID IT!!!

Now You're Leading!

You've just completed navigating the first steps of a powerful 30+ day journey—one filled with insight, development, and real progress—that will keep moving forward.

Whether you're stepping into leadership for the first time or are focused on leveling up your impact, you've done the most important thing a leader can do:

You showed up.

You asked questions. You got curious. You listened. You practiced. You learned. You tried. You failed. You got up. You adapted. You never gave up. That's what sets you apart.

Leaders don't need to have all the answers; their strength lies in their willingness to learn openly and continuously.

Keep finding joy in the messy and meaningful work of leadership. People need you; they need your gifts.

This is just the beginning. Stay curious, stay human, and lead with heart. You're just getting started.

A PERSONAL NOTE FROM RAISA

Leadership is a lifelong practice and you're off to a strong start. You'll start to learn so much from others, adapting best practices and evolving the process.

I wrote this book because I believe first-time managers deserve accessible support, encouragement, and practical tools that make leadership feel attainable. While some managers are fortunate to have great resources at their disposal, many emerging leaders don't have the genuine support they truly need.

Leadership can't be tackled in thirty days. Lessons aren't applied in 5 weeks; we know that. When you feel stuck, carve out small bites. Don't eat the whole chocolate cake in one sitting. Keep revisiting what you learned. As your experience deepens, the content will speak to you differently.

Growth is a daily choice. You've taken the first steps to become the kind of leader people will remember in all the right ways. Make it your intention to be the answer to someone's question, concern, or prayer.

Your team is lucky to have you.

Raisa

Raisa M. Ramos, MBA, SHRM-CP
HR Advisor & Leadership Coach
Find Joy Off the Path, LLC

KEEP GROWING WITH RAISA

Imagine transforming into a respected leader who reduces employee turnover and builds a high-performing culture...

More than that, you will increase your **CONFIDENCE** so that you can navigate tough conversations, inspire your team, and lead with purpose from day one.

Visit **findjoyoffthepath.com/book-now-youre-leading** to purchase the book, gain access to free resources, templates, and more!

Become a Client Now: Work With Raisa

Are you ready to design a leadership strategy that works?

My commitment to businesses is to design services that meet leaders and organizations wherever they are in their growth.

Schedule your consultation at calendly.com/raisafindjoyoffthepath or raisa@findjoyoffthepath.com to learn how working together will elevate your results.

As an engineer turned HR leader, companies hire me to reduce HR headaches, strengthen leadership, and make sure employees feel informed and valued. Here are 3 main ways we can work together:

1. Fractional HR services, so you don't need a full-time hire to get real HR support that keeps your business running smoothly.
2. Spanish HR translations, especially during open enrollment, so every employee understands their benefits and feels included.
3. Speaking events, leadership workshops and coaching that turns overwhelmed managers into confident leaders without excessively pulling them away from fast-paced industries. If you're looking to bring an expert motivator directly to your people that will inspire your leaders to build high-performing, impactful cultures, Raisa is who you want to invite!

Let's connect about how these services can make your business stronger.

All services are available in English & Español.

Website: www.findjoyoffthepath.com
Email: raisa@findjoyoffthepath.com

Let's connect:

LinkedIn: linkedin.com/in/raisamramos
Instagram: @raisa.m.ramos
Facebook: https://www.facebook.com/findjoyoffthepath

ACKNOWLEDGEMENTS

This book came to life with the love, encouragement, and support of many people, and I am deeply grateful.

To my husband Chris, and children, Carlos and Alex—thank you for your unconditional love. You are my inspiration and why I strive to find joy off the path every day.

To my parents, Awilda and Luis, and family, who instilled in me the values of faith, grit, and perseverance—your example has shaped every step of my path.

To the mentors, colleagues, and leaders I've had the privilege to learn from over the years—your wisdom, challenges, and encouragement inspired the lessons within these pages. A special thank you to the teams I've had the privilege to lead; you were my teachers in what leadership truly means.

To my village, who always showed up for me and supported this project – you encouragement keeps me moving forward: Carlos, Carmichelle, Carolyn, Edna, Joanly, Jody, Juan, Julia, María Elena, Melissa J., Melissa S., Sandy, Tere, Tracy, Yaritza, Yazmín;

And to those who supported this book behind the scenes—editors, reviewers, and creative partners—thank you for your expertise and helping me bring this vision to life.

Most of all, thank you to every new manager stepping into leadership. This book is for you.

REFERENCES

Hanson, T., & Hanson, B. Z. (1995). Who Will Do What by When?: How to Use Accountability to Get the Job Done. Jossey-Bass.

www.ingramcontent.com/pod-product-compliance
Lightning Source LLC
Chambersburg PA
CBHW070634030426
42337CB00020B/4010